Behind THE Mirror

26 EXTRAORDINARY JOURNEYS

Thank you for your support!
I'm hoping you will be blessed
inspired + empowered

TI' SHA LOVING-WILLIAMS

Ti' Sha Loving Williams

outskirts press

Outskirts Press, Inc.
http://www.outskirtspress.com

ISBN: 978-1-9772-3401-8

Outskirts Press and the "OP" logo are trademarks belonging to Outskirts Press, Inc.

PRINTED IN THE UNITED STATES OF AMERICA

ACKNOWLEDGEMENTS

First, I would like to acknowledge and thank my mother for being the best mother in the world. I would like to dedicate this book to Cynthia Loving and my Grandmother Geneva Loving Hitchens.

To my handsome and intelligent son Daymon, you are my light in my darkest hour. You give me the courage to face obstacles when I think it's not possible. Di'Maya, you are my beautiful, intelligent princess, and your caring and loving heart gives me the strength to continue each day. You are my heartbeat! To my husband, Keith Williams, you are the rock and foundation of our family. I love you, and thanks so much for letting me be who I am.

To all of the 25 women in this book, I love each and everyone one of you, and I couldn't ask for better friends and family. You are the reason this book exists. Your strength and friendship continues to guide me.

To my brother Bobby Ferguson and my sisters Yvette Sutton and Chiquita Sparks, the three of you are the best brother and sisters that anyone could ask for. My brothers-in-law and sister-in-law Mark Williams, Maria Williams, Gregory Williams, Laura Ferguson, Gina Williams, Michael Williams, and family. To Grand Myrtle Ross and my nieces and nephews Tanika Livingston & Rick Livingston (Trey), Christoper Williams, Laura Ferguson, Melissa Ferguson, Adam & Aaron Ferguson, Nicola Sparks, Brandon & Kayla Waller, Brandi & Abe Martha (Evelyn), Khalin Sparks, Asa Sparks, Kaneetha Holmes & Monica Akpotosevwe, Christa Loving, Camille Loving, Errol & Sarah Williams - Wint, (Averi) & (Amara), Marcus Williams (Alana), Jayden,

Za' Mya, The twins Kehlani & Saniyah.

Special thanks to Dana Loving Swain (Chanzler & Paris), Tonie Loving (Kaden), Diana Loving, TK Williams, Alex Williams, Nicole Williams, Keith Barksdale, Ricky Barksdale, Panama Benton, Eric Smith, Kim Dunn, Kierra, Kash, Melody Boards (Janya & Shayla). Special thanks to my Uncles and Aunts: Uncle Christopher Loving and Aunt Carla Loving, Aunt Cecilia Loving Cromwell, Uncle Gregory Loving, Uncle Donald Loving, Aunt Mary Margaret Richardson, Uncle Marlon Cromwell, Yvonne Roundtree Robinson, and Denise Langford. My great friends Terra Nixon, Linda Love, Kyra Walker, Lori Long, Oscar Coleman Jr. Jeffrey James and Family, Chef Lon Durbin, Kim Lapean and Family, The Parakeet Café' Family, Robin Proctor Martin, Marlissa Smith, Alene Denning, Joe Denning, Heather Cherrington & Family GA, The Gatewood Family, The Gillaspie Family North Carolina, The Millsap Family North Carolina, The Scott Family North Carolina, The Parks Family North Carolina, Freddie and Leslie Morrison, The Barksdale Family Nashville Tennessee, The Robertson Family Columbus Ohio, Anthony & Marci Holt (A2) Nashville TN, Anthony & Tamara Bowles, Marshall & Sonya Gray, Bethany Smith & Family, Bertha Hunter, and Pastor Samuel K. Hunter, The Next Level Church Bowling Green Kentucky, US Bank Consumer Direct Team Bowling Green and Owensboro Kentucky. To the great photographers that captured the essence of all of our Girl Trips and fun photoshoots. Thank you to each one of the photographers for seeing my vision and creating such a beautiful legacy for me to share with the world. Each of you are beyond talented and I value your creativity.

Abby Photo Mandeville Louisiana http://abbyphoto.com/

K-Marie Photography Ketrina Myers Marion Kentucky

OH Photography Oscar Herrera Costa Rica oscarherrera.net

Carver Photography Vickie Carver Bowling Green Kentucky vickie196928@gmail.com

Javier Olivero Photography Puerto Rico www.javierolivero.com

Amy Vaughn Photography Bowling Green, Kentucky

IN MEMORY

My brother Dewayne Sparks, Mother In Law Bertie Williams, Sister in law Brenda Williams, LeSonya, Aunt Alice Gordon, Uncle Henry Gordon, Great Granddaddy Pappy Barksdale, Aunt Ethel Bunton (aka Sister) Godfather Mr. Bill Walker, Grandfather C. Holder Loving, Aunt Gladys Barksdale, Uncle Spencer Barksdale, Step-Grandfather Hicey Ross, Billy Joe Loving, Marvin Loving, Aunt Fannie Mildred Loving, Uncle Robert Loving, Mose Lee Loving, Pearline Kirby, Eleanor Reeves, Harold Bradshaw, Reverend Ella Parks, James Parks, Dr. Neresa Minatrea, Father In Law Charles Williams, Charles Barksdale, Ed Dansereau, Ruth Cat Robertson, Caroyln Hayes, Michael Rives, Farmer & Jane Rowe, Nathaniel Robertson, Claudia Burnam, Uncle Richard Manning, Aunt Johnnie Ridley, Aunt Loretta Grady, Uncle Waldo Grady, Marci Woodruff, John Bolling (JB), Robert Braeden Combs, Mrs. Lavinia Gatewood, Joe Scott, Nedra Smith, William Patton, Montoyia Boards and Baby Giana.

JOURNEY 1

Today, being the day you decided to read this book, is one of the most uplifting moments in my life, and hopefully, it will go on to make a big difference in your life! I'm inspired that I can share my journey, and I hope that it will lift you up, open your eyes to new beginnings and give you that exhilarating feeling that "Dreams Do Come True". I'm bringing a different twist to empowerment through several different women from all walks of life. These women have lifted, inspired, loved, and, most of all, empowered me throughout my life. In this book, you may choose to read it all at once or read each journey per day. You will be able to understand the POWER you hold within yourself and explore it along with the spirit and gift you were given to share with the world. I've decided to share my journey because I finally understand my gift for helping others. It clicked and made sense that I can be great at anything, I put my mind to. It's all about the mindset to conquer those things and, most importantly, 'IF' you want to accomplish certain goals. My very first realization was that "I'm here for a reason!" God makes no mistakes! Now it's up to me to understand where I fit into the puzzle of making a difference in the world along with being happy while making that difference.

Each person has a story to tell that's just as powerful and beautiful as the person sitting next to you. Through sharing the experiences in your life, whether it's bad or good, you can pay it forward and help the load be a little lighter for the next generation. Many people have helped me through my life to overcome obstacles in my path. My desire is to lift you, show that anything is possible, and give you that feeling of hope and encouragement. To actualize this process, I have

25 journeys to share with you from all walks of life that helped me write this powerful book just for you. I call these remarkable women, my friends, neighbors, mothers, doctors, caregivers, entrepreneurs, lawyers, sisters, daughters, but most importantly my family. This book is in journey submissions, not chapters. The reason I wanted to share these stories with you is that these are ordinary women who have extraordinary journeys to share. It is impossible to know what others have been through, but only if you share experiences will you find out that you are not alone. I will start with the person who gave life to me and share a little bit of her journey.

The only name that I will reveal at this time will be the first journey in this book. Her name is 'Cynthia Anne Loving' and true to her name; she happened to be a loving Mother. You will get a glimpse into the beginning of my life and the most important women therein before reading about my journey. I assure you without a doubt that you will be inspired!

My mother was born in a small city called Bowling Green, Kentucky. Yes, it's called Bowling Green, the home of the Bluegrass, Corvette Plant/Museum, and Western Kentucky University. Those are just a few of the things we are known for in Bowling Green, Kentucky. Although we weren't much in number, we were a strong community. We are located about 1 ½ hour from Louisville, Kentucky, where most people are familiar with either the Kentucky Derby, University of Louisville or the recent death and injustice of Breonna Taylor. We are also about 45 minutes away from Nashville Tennessee, which is the Country Music Capital. Bowling Green is a small town, but continues to be a growing and thriving community with a current population of around 68,000.

I started my journey from the beautiful state of Kentucky, in an affectionate Christian home with great values, a hardworking family, and intelligent women with strong leadership skills. As my journey is revealed throughout this book, you will see why all of these strong women have helped to mold me into the person, I've become today. Most people see friendships in terms of the people they have chosen to be friends with and their relationship with them. I, on the other hand, view it a little differently; my belief is that the people that are good for you will come into your life and will eventually be good for your mind, body, and soul. These women have contributed to my growth in many ways. All of the women in this book were chosen to be in my life. As the world turns daily, you will run into people you might interact with for just 5 minutes but will teach you valuable lessons and give you powerful information. One of the biggest things we fail to do is **STOP** and **LISTEN**. We are always busy running from one place to another, working long hours, caring for loved ones so much that we sometimes don't take the time to slow down and LISTEN. It's the simple things that could change your life or lead you in the right direction of your gift. No matter the color of your skin, gender, religion, language, education, finance, etc. We all have something to offer and should always have a positive impact on someone's life. I learned all of these as a young child from my mother, who is so strong, powerful, wise, and intelligent beyond her years. She remains a most generous person and one of the most open-minded people you'll ever meet. My mother taught me values that I hope to transfer to my children.

She was 16 years old when I was conceived, and at that time, she was top of her class in high school. Unlike today's world, it was much different in 1969. People didn't have an openmind about a pregnant and unmarried 16-year-old black girl. My mother, who's also known as "Anne," prepared her life so I could enter into this world. All through the duration of her pregnancy, she had it very difficult.

She was being raised by my Great Aunt, 'Ethel Elizabeth Bunton' and my Great, Great Grandfather, 'George Washington Barksdale'. My Grandmother, 'Geneva B. Hitchens' and Grandfather, 'C. Holder Loving' were both ill and unable to take care of my mother due to their mental illness. Of course, no one wanted to speak of this illness because no one understood mental illness back in those days. My grandparents were victims of this sort of treatment and had to deal with people who did not understand their illness. My Great Aunt Ethel did a great job filling the shoes for my grandmother and grandfather while they were in and out of hospitals. She tried to do the best she could to help raise my mother. My Great Grandfather George was up in age, but he still tried to help when possible too. Once my mother started showing signs of pregnancy, she wasn't allowed to attend school, and from what I was told by family members, it didn't seem to bother her. She continued to prepare for my arrival and also continued to focus on returning to school. My Great Aunt would tell me that my mother ate plenty of vegetables, fruits and drank a lot of milk each day (my mother had read that fruits and vegetables were things that would help in having a healthy pregnancy). Throughout the gestation period, she continued to prepare for my arrival. Finally, I was born on Easter Sunday, April 6, 1969, after she'd gone through 24 hours of labor. She would later tell me that she remembered being scared and not knowing exactly what to expect. The nurses were not as kind to her because they looked down on her for a couple of reasons. One of which was the fact that she was a black girl and another being that she was having a baby at a young age out of wedlock. There were times when she would hear whispers from the nurses talking about her while she was in labor. Again, those comments probably stayed with her, but instead of breaking her down, it only made her stronger. Before I was born, my mother was already proud of me. After a few weeks of recovery, she returned to work and prepared to return to school in the fall. Once school started, she skipped a grade to catch up with her classmates and still continued to be at the top of her class. My mother was very intelligent and grasped whatever she was taught in no time. A lot of the neighbors in our community would always ask her advice or help. At the time, we lived in a black community, and each family was involved in making sure we succeeded in life. The number one focus for my mother was taking care of me and making sure that I was well cared for as I grew up. After graduating from high school, she proceeded to attend Western Kentucky University. Our family felt she had the intelligence and deserved to attend college just like they planned before my arrival. My mother had a lot of determination and knew that she needed a better job in order to support us, along with the goal of fulfilling her dream of being the first to graduate in our family. Times were hard, especially with money for tuition and raising a two-year-old. My mother needed help with buying books for college but couldn't afford to pay for the books after paying for tuition. Like most determined students who couldn't afford to buy books, my mother took notes in class and went to class without books! For me, it's a testimony that you can achieve anything in life if you are able to block out negative roadblocks and find the alternative route to success. Fast forward to four years of college, I was now five years old, my mother was about to graduate from Western Kentucky University with honors 'Summa Cum Laude' without having books for her classes and working full time at Hardees? It was a most impressive achievement given the circumstance! My mother opted for milk, diapers, clothes, and helping the family instead of buying books for school. I struggle today to take good notes during my meetings at work. I only take notes in order to retain information to share with my team. So, everything that my mother did I watched it very closely. I remember sitting at Western Kentucky University with my Great Aunt Ethel watching my mother accept her diploma. My mother really wanted my Great Great Grandfather to be there, but he had passed away before seeing her graduate. I remember smiling and watching her in a black cap and robe walking into the arena. Even though I didn't understand why everyone was dressed alike, I understood that it was a very big deal. I knew this was a great moment, and she did all of this while taking care of me, working full-time, and going to school without books. After the graduation ceremony, we greeted my mother, and we were so excited and happy. My mother leaned down to me and gave me the tassel from her cap. To this day, I still feel that was one of my greatest moments ever, a feeling that only increased as I grew older and understood what it really meant to my mother and our entire family. Having graduated, she went in search of a career in teaching. My mother taught me to reach for goals, no matter how high. Keep my head up while I walk. Make direct eye contact at all times with whoever I was having a conversation with. Some days, I still struggle with keeping my head up, but I hear my mother's voice in my ear, and when I do, I'd hold my head as high up as possible.

As a child, I grew tall so fast that I was easily the tallest one in class, so much so that I wished to be shorter, and I would always walk with my head down (which annoyed my mother a lot). It was totally against the things she'd taught me such as: you must always look up; you should always know how to speak to people and carry on a conversation no matter who you are speaking to in any situation; write daily goals down and mark them off as you accomplish them at the end of the day and then set new goals; practice speaking in front of a mirror to build confidence which will help you be able to speak to groups of people. My mother would always say, "Look in the mirror and believe in that person staring back at you". When I looked into the mirror, she would say, "Don't you want to know more about that person, "Behind the Mirror"? And this brings me back to the reason I put this book together. I want to not only share my journey but also share the journeys of some of the people that helped me grow as a mother, daughter, wife, sister, colleague, and, most of all, as a friend. You will quickly find that some of my friends have great advice capable of getting you through a bad day. Some of them can tell you about their journeys from an ordinary standpoint. Everyday, people want to know that someone just like them went through the same struggles, but overcame those obstacles in their lives. I enjoy reality television and watch a lot of those shows for entertainment, but the friendships that I have formed over my life are long-lasting, uplifting, and positive. I have acquainted myself with people whose ultimate desire is to lift each other up. Often, we find that we see other people who are doing great things in their life, and we try to find something negative. Our mindset should always be to look for the positive in another person first before the thought even enters our mind to pick out something negative. We need to train our minds to change our way of thinking. Basically, don't judge a book by its cover.

Just as changing to a healthy lifestyle, you also must change your mind. Don't just change your way of eating to change your lifestyle; put your brain on a healthy lifestyle. If you remain positive or find something positive in every negative situation, it will become a habit. Start with your mind, and the rest will follow!

Now, it's time to introduce you to some strong, intelligent, beautiful, wise, and uplifting friends and family that you can relate to and also learn from in your own journey.

JOURNEY 2

I am 40 years old and currently working as the Insurance Coordinator for a Dental Care Office. I love my job; I love my boss and my co-workers. In our dental office, we are often able to help alleviate pain and/or give a patient a reason to smile. Some people go for years without smiling, and being able to help them smile again is a great reward.

One thing I'm very proud of is my salvation; I became a Christian at the age of 11. I am also proud that I went to college and graduated with an Associate's Degree in Business. When I started college in the fall of 1996, I was miserably shy. I had been shy most of my life and was very self-conscious and never wanted any attention. When I graduated 3 years later, one of my co-workers told me I was a different person, that I'd gained a lot of confidence during my college years, and she could see the change. I guess for me that at college, you didn't see as many cliques as in high-school; there wasn't really an in-crowd, and if there was, it wasn't so obvious. Everybody just kind of did their own thing, and nobody cared that much if you were different.

After college, I started full-time work, but I was still missing out on something that I wanted very badly. I have always wanted to be a wife and mother. I dated here and there, but not anything serious for the most part, and then I met someone. At first, it seemed that I had hit the jackpot... he was handsome and funny and hardworking, and he seemed crazy about me. That lasted only until I did or said something that he didn't like. Our relationship was rocky, to say the least; he was mean and had severe anger issues. Everything that went wrong was somehow my fault, and he was constantly trying to control how I did things so that it would make him happy. That tumultuous relationship went off and on for over three years. Finally, it was over, but I was broken. He had made me question everything about myself. He told me that no man would ever want me. It took a long time for me to get over that relationship. I got some very good advice from friends and family, and eventually, I just got comfortable being single. I took on the attitude that I was not going to settle and that if I couldn't find someone that would treat me like I deserved, then I would just stay single. I was happy with being me; I didn't need a man to define me. I have to say that at times my patience wore very thin, but after several years of just being me, happy and doing what I wanted; when I wanted, I finally met the "guy for me" … We met online and immediately hit it off, it was like he got me and I got him, and all of the stuff that we had each experienced in the past had made us appreciate each other even more. We only dated about six months before we got engaged and married six months after. I was 35 when I got married, but I tell everybody that I wouldn't change our story. It was worth everything that I had gone through in the past to have someone who loved me hands down no matter what. I tell younger girls/women all of the time to just enjoy being you, enjoy school, work, etc. Don't rush into anything. A relationship does not define you; it is way more than that.

I am bipolar. I was diagnosed in 2007, and it is an illness I was scared of because my Dad and Grandfather had it and did not set good examples of living with it. Neither of them took their medicine, went to therapy, or anything else that they should have. It took me a while, but I came to terms with the illness. I take my medication every single day and will until the day that I die. This is just part of living with the illness, and to me, a little pill is worth my sanity. This illness doesn't define me and is only a small part of who I am.

I have been blessed with amazing friends and family that have always been there for me. They have lifted me up during the good and bad times. My journey is a continual one... it's had mountains, and it's had valleys.

Yet, it's in the valley that God teaches us how to appreciate those times when we are on the mountain.

JOURNEY 3

My life was forever changed when I was involved in a car accident at the age of 21 in 1996. This singular event drastically altered the course of my life. If you saw the damage from the wreckage, you'd not expect anything to come from it. The car was repaired and was fine, but my health was another story. I developed chronic migraines and muscle spasms and was left to deal with daily pain. For the next 5 years, I literally lived in the Dr.'s office and the ER. It was day after day in pain for me, but I went to great lengths to be able to continue working. At my worst, I would spend my lunch hour sleeping in my car, so I could make it through the rest of the day at work. Finally, I lost my job because of how much work I had missed. It devastated me; I have had a migraine for a solid month without a break. If you have ever had one for just one day, you and only you, know that pain. I spent 5 years trying to find a Dr. who knew what was going on and could help me. I knew the accident was the cause of my issues. Because nothing showed up on any tests, treatment was non-existent. I was told so many horrible things from people who doctors like, "There is nothing wrong with you", "You are making it up", "You will never get better", and the worst was, "You are just doing it to get insurance money". Yes, those idiots were a one time only Dr. visit! That was the farthest from the truth from who I am and a huge insult! I spent many rounds of hospitalizations trying to get things under control to no avail. Finally, in 2000, I found a clinic in Ann Arbor, Michigan, that specialized in migraines. They have been the answer to many prayers.

There, I was like all other patients instead of one who they had never seen so bad! Yes, this was from the car accident! Yes, I could get better! There they helped me to get better, but the quality of life was still very poor. I was still down with a migraine 3-5 days a week. I was on disability. I approved the first time. That shows how poor my health was. I went through numerous procedures to ease the muscle spasms from Botox, nerve blocks, nerve ablation, trigger point injections, and finally, an occipital nerve stimulator implant. I was told I would never work again. I proved them wrong. I volunteered for 1 year to gain my strength back. I was an employee for 1 year until my health declined, and once again, I had to quit. That was in 2004. In 2011, I was introduced to Zija. That product has changed my life! Over the past 3 years, I have been able to come off all meds but one. I am thrilled to say my migraines are now a thing of the past. It has been almost a year since I have had one. In January of this year, I began working part-time again and in August 2014, full-time. I was always determined that I would be back on my feet, taking care of myself again! God used me to prepare me for what was ahead. Our story is all part of our journey. My life has been completely changed. I've experienced things in my 20's that most people never do. My outlook on life is so much different. I'm so thankful for each and every day that I can get up and go. I'm blessed to be at a job that I love. I have people in my life I love. Most of all, I'm blessed with health. I'm sharing my story in hopes of helping others that are experiencing chronic pain to know there is something that could help. There is light at the end of the tunnel. Our journey only makes us stronger. God chose me to help others, and that is my mission. I love seeing people get their life back! I hope my story can be of inspiration to you or to someone you know and love. Please read the update at the end of the book.

Behind The Mirror

JOURNEY 4

I've worked at 440 Main Restaurant, for 17 years, and all of my time at 440 has been with the current owners. I'm considered their right-hand person because I've worked with them for so long. As an 'Events Coordinator', my responsibilities include large party details and reservations for the banquet rooms and catering. I oversee all catering and specials events that take place outside of 440 Main, including weddings, private Holiday dinner parties, Chamber of Commerce "Business After Hours" and local fundraising events such as "The Taste of BG." I also book live music for the bar, and I handle the social media, which is an ever-changing job, trying to keep up with the latest media trends.

I enjoy my job because I work for a family-owned restaurant; the owners have watched me grow from a college student to a married woman and a mother. The relationship I have with them is unique, and I consider myself blessed. An additional bonus to my job is the fact that I am able to participate in people's memorable occasions, as an intricate part of wedding receptions, anniversaries, retirements, and birthdays. It's a wonderful honor to be trusted with these important life events.

I am a proud mother of 2 wonderful boys: Edward Wyatt Goshorn IV (he goes by Walker), aged 14, and James Gunnar Goshorn (he goes by Gunnar), aged 10.

Thinking of myself, I am immensely pleased with my continued ability to evolve as a woman; I try new things and push myself outside of my comfort zone. For example, I had never been a "runner," but in 2011, I decided I was going to run. I participated in my first 5K in March 2011; in October 2011, I ran a 10K; in April 2012, I ran a 10-mile race in Louisville. In November 2013, I ran my first half-marathon (13.2 miles.); I ran another half-marathon in 2014. In November of 2015, I ran a full marathon in Puerto Rico.

I enjoy to run in the morning; on average, I exercise four to five days a week, including running, stationary bike, and weights. I like the time to myself; I am a better wife, mom, and person when I get that time to breathe, clear my head, and focus on myself. I feel strong when I sweat, and it encourages me to make better food decisions throughout my day.

I need to stop obessing about every single piece of food I put in my mouth. Every piece of food equals praise or scorn. It's ridiculous. The pressure for that praise or scorn comes completely from my own inner monologue. All I can say is this; I'm a work in progress. Ultimately, the number on the scale does not dictate my worth.

Body image has always been a factor in my life for as long as I can remember. My weight has been my cross to bear. I was never the petite girl; I started wearing a bra in the 5th grade. Throughout my adult life, I have been a yo-yo on the scale. When I run and exercise regularly, I feel capable and accomplished. When I sweat, I feel strong. Currently, I'm in a good place. I've lost some weight in the past few months. I've been committed to exercise, and I'm using an application on my smartphone to log calories, portions, exercise, and weight goals. The app is called "Lose It." And this is the first time I have ever kept a food journal, logging every single thing I eat. I've read several times that a food journal is an excellent way to become aware of portions/calories. I have to say about that, "it has worked for me so far. It keeps me conscious of my food and drink decisions."

Blessed to be healthy right now, I have one ovary as a result of a large cyst on that ovary. I have a scar on my breast, the result of the removal of a non-cancerous cyst. Thankfully, the health incidents that I have incurred haven't left me without any permanent damage.

My dreams right now involve seeing my boys grow into healthy men and seeing their stories unfold. I also dream of the time when it will only be my husband and me alone in our home. The few "couple" time we get for ourselves right now is quite scarce, but I know it won't always be that way. I look forward to us rediscovering each other, continuing the adventure we started together so long ago.

I used to run with doubt, but now she can't keep up!

JOURNEY 5

I was 16 when I was raped by a family member. At the time of the incident, I was a virgin. As a result of it, I got pregnant, opted to have the baby, and do the best I could in raising her. At the time of her birth, I experienced extreme postpartum depression and contemplated suicide. I felt as though I was alone. The guy I was dating at the time not only stayed with me, but he let me know he was in it for the long haul.

I then prayed more and asked for guidance. I quickly came to terms with the fact that "this child" had not asked to be here anymore than I had asked for the events that led to this difficult moment in my life. I was blessed enough to have a lot of support as well as help from close friends and family members. I did a lot of counseling and came to terms with speaking about what happened to me. I no longer looked at myself as a victim. I began to see myself as a survivor.

I now deem myself as a positive force and a mentor to others who may have experienced the same hurdles.

Ladies, please know that in crisis, you have to find that motivating force to get you back on your feet and moving forward. This can only be accomplished by first telling yourself that whatever happened isn't your fault. Talk to someone; vent every chance you get because that's also a source of therapy.

Through prayer and the grace of GOD, I learned to love my daughter just like a child that was planned and conceived out of love. She is the fire that ignites my every move and every decision to be a better and stronger individual. She is strong, smart, determined, sensitive, beautiful, and compassionate. My daughter is now a 21-year old young woman living life as someone her age should. She is now a senior in college and on her way to becoming a nursing-practitioner. She is the diamond that came from a very rough situation.

During my journey, I have also overcome other significant events in my life, but my advice to our young adults would be thus:

Take care of yourself first. Don't ever depend on any man to take care of or validate you. Have an amazing sense of self and maneuvering through the trials in life will be a little easier.

JOURNEY 6

I am not the best at expressing myself on paper, but I'm going to try and do my best. As I reflect on my life, I feel as though I have cast a shadow of encouragement. As I journey through this thing called life, I can honestly say that I try to get along with all I come in contact with. I give a smile or a hug even if I don't know you. A smile is the best way to connect. Hey, we all smile in the same language, and we understand, for the most part, what a smile means. We need to find time to get to know people.

If we could look into the life of the most hateful and mean spirited person, we will be able to see why they are that way. The same goes for the most positive person. If we take time to get to know people, we might get a glimpse of the reason for their "being". As I journey, I am learning that time really is a luxury. We think we have so much of it when in reality, in fact, we have so little. This is why our time should be used to be all that God has created us to be. God's timing is everything. You are God's creation. Ask God to help you be a good steward of your time and God's time.

During my journey, I was blessed with the opportunity to be a kinder-garten teacher. Here are some of my responsibilities in the classroom:

Guide the learning process toward the achievement of curriculum goals and establishes objectives for all lessons, units, projects, and the like in order to communicate these objectives to students and parents. Assists the administration in implementing board policies, administrative regulations, and school rules governing student life and conduct, develop reasonable rules of classroom behavior and procedure and maintain order in the classroom in a fair and just manner. Also, a doctor, lawyer, social worker, and psychologist, just to name a few. What I love about my job is that it is truly a ministry! I love seeing the growth that occurs in my little ones, and I love cultivating the kind of learner they are so that they can reach their God-given potential. I know that I help to provide a strong voice for the voiceless.

Of the things I'm most proud of, finishing two degrees stand out. One degree I finished after the birth of my first child when he was only 6-months old. The second degree (which is a master's degree) I completed when he was 4 years of age. I have had the opportunity to not only visit out of the country but was able to live and attend school out of the country.

Some of my past illness consists of a broken pelvis and fractured hip. I was hit by a drunk driver on New Year's Eve, 1994, and was bedridden for 6 months. I had to learn to walk again. This time allowed me to reflect on my life, and I became closer to God. During this time, I read a lot of my Bible and begin to pray more. Currently, I'm a survivor and prayer warrior against my current illness, which is a pituitary tumor and mitral valve regurgitation. The fact that God takes what we consider to be a long time does not mean that God is not at work in our lives. It is difficult to journey through life without God.

She loves to see people happy

Has to try her best to look and be her best

Aspire to change the world, one child, at a time

Shining light upon all who see

Hopeful that one day she will live out her dreams

Running the race that has beset before me

Ancestors are the reason for my being

Yokes are being broken right now

JOURNEY 7

My journey begins being a daughter from a single mother home. We didn't have a lot of money, but we had each other, and faith in God, along with a supported extended family, helped us make it during those times. My mother married a man when I was very young, and the marriage was less than ideal, to put it mildly. My childhood was not the easiest, but we made it through. I look back and wonder how we made it, and the only explanation that makes sense was God's grace, protection, and mercy. I wouldn't trade my experience because it made me who I am today. I am fiercely protective of my loved ones, especially children. It also made me appreciate my life in all of the ups and downs to not take anything for granted. I am a living testimony that you can do all things through Christ. Today I'm married and have a wonderful son that I love dearly. If the Lord is willing, I still have a long journey ahead of me, and I'm looking forward to what is in store for me next.

JOURNEY 8

The Long, Dark Tunnel

The story, "The Silence is Deafening" could have been my story. While I was reading the book, it occurred to me that I, too, was on my way to being discharged from the hospital at one point, and the fact that my blood pressure (BP) spiked probably saved my life. It not only spiked but remained high and erratic. Lucky me! Thankfully, my story had a different ending to Joan's. My heart goes out to her husband and family. The loss of this woman is a tragedy.

My experience taught me many things, the least of which was the duality of life. Until this happened, I had a very naive understanding of life. As this story doesn't easily unfold, it's difficult to write. There is no linear, logical progression to this story. It is a tangled, messy web of intersecting events, information, and people going in every direction all at once. It has taken me five years just to process it and come to the mental clarity to make this attempt.

At the beginning of this story, my daughter and I are one. Her life needed my womb for survival. I needed her survival to be worthy of life. My physical life depended on becoming two, my soul's life depended on giving all and nurturing this one, new life. But somewhere in this story, as is inevitable in all pregnancies, one becomes two. If this is all too melodramatic for you, I agree. But there it is. This is very hard to talk about, but I feel I must.

In addition, I must disagree with Todd on one point. I don't believe that doctors refuse to admit the existence of this disease. It may appear so because we are dependent on doctors to guide us through the effects of this stealthy and vicious disease. Rather, I believe that non-medical entities have too much control over the doctors who are caring for patients attacked by the disease. The mainstream, the usual, the odds, determine the path of least resistance to the highest profits in every business. The art of medicine, intended to be crafted to the individual, is drowned by an overwhelming flow of mass production crafted for the majority of people for the business of medicine. Unfortunately for Joan, she received the "one size fits most" version of medicine and paid with her life. Fortunately for me, I received a tailor-made version of medicine and escaped with my life. The medical community calls the former "cookbook medicine," and they despise it. But they participate in it and perpetuate it because they are forced by economic reality. This is another tangled, messy web of intersecting events, information, and people.

I want to take this opportunity to thank my doctor for her skill as well as her humility. She carried me as far as she was able, and then wisely turned my case over to others when she reached the limits of her knowledge and experience. Kudos to her! This is the ideal way to practice medicine. I owe everything to her and to my nurses. She was brave enough and strong enough to say, in front of her team, her patient and her community of colleagues, "I don't know" and to ask for help.

The Long, Dark Tunnel is a turning point in my life. I entered, was consumed, changed forever, and released from the tunnel over a span of 9 days. The tunnel cleaves my memories and existence into 'before' and 'after'.

At 30 weeks of pregnancy, 10 weeks before my due date, I had just had a baby shower. My husband and I had traveled to central Kentucky that weekend to his hometown for the event. I wasn't feeling well, my vision in one eye was blurry and dim, and my feet were swollen to the point that I couldn't wear regular shoes. Everyone that I talked to assured me that the swelling was normal. I was determined not to be a wimp and to function normally in my job and my life through the last trimester. I wanted to conserve my leave time for use once my daughter was born.

Monday morning came, and I got up to get ready for work. I soon realized that my vision in both eyes was now limited. When I looked directly at my husband, all I could see was his silhouette. I could see things in my peripheral vision, but not directly in front of me. My husband wanted me to call my doctor. I planned to, but I had to leave for work at 6:45 am; the doctor's office begins to accept calls at 8:30 am. As I got ready, I remembered that it was my week to drive the carpool. So, I called my friends and asked if someone else could drive since I was not able to see. My friends were alarmed. They wanted me to see the doctor, and I promised I would call my doctor as soon as the office opened. I should mention as well that I am hearing impaired. Not being able to see people when they talked severely limited my ability to understand what was said to me and to communicate effectively.

My difficulty in communicating became very apparent once I got to the office. I realized just how much I relied on reading lips. My stress was mounting because I needed to work. My job was to collect medical malpractice insurance claims data for my state, compile it and report to the state legislative body by September 1. My due date was September 28. It was July 18, and my work and plans for the next month simply did not allow for this distraction. I called the doctor as soon as her office opened and asked if I should just call an eye doctor. They asked me to come into the office, and then they would refer me to the eye doctor if necessary. Ugh, that wasn't as efficient as I had hoped. My supervisor offered to drive me to the doctor since I had not been able to drive to work. I had a bad feeling that something was wrong, and I called my husband and asked him to meet me at the doctor's office. I was feeling foolish and wimpy by the time my husband got there, and we went to the examination room. It's normal for pregnant women to feel weird, tired, and uncomfortable, right? I was afraid they would put me on bed rest. I did not have time for that. The nurse took my BP, and even though I couldn't see her, I could tell she was a little unnerved. She asked for a urine sample and then told me to go to a small room with a recliner in it. She had me lay back in it on my left side. I remember thinking, "this is nice, but I don't really have time for this." She told me to lay there and try to relax, and she would be back in ten minutes. I tried to, but I thought that I really wanted them to figure out what was wrong with my eyes so I could get back to work. I could feel every minute of my leave time ticking away as I sat there.

After my little rest, my BP was taken again, and it had not improved, so I was shown into the examination room to wait for the doctor. The nurse again had me lay on my left side. My doctor came in and told us that I had preeclampsia with high levels of protein in my urine and very high BP. She was admitting me to the hospital, and I would have my baby within the next 48 hours. It was shocking to hear this. It was too early to deliver the baby. I still had two and a half months! Ten weeks! We didn't have a nursery set up at home. My very organized, concerned, and methodical husband offered helpfully that we had not yet had the birthing class and that we were in no way prepared. The doctor smiled and good-naturedly responded that was quite alright; anything they were going to teach us was not going to apply anyay. There went all of my carefully laid out plans. I was trying to find out who I could call and describe my work. I was still figuring out the procedure myself; I sure didn't have a manual I could just hand over. I was letting everyone down. I now offered bed rest as a preferred alternative to delivering the baby too early. The answer was a very definite "no". The delivery of the baby was the only cure for this disease. And so began the worst and best week of our lives.

From this point on, most of this story is a blur to me. I've pieced it together from my random memories, friends' accounts, my husband's recollection, and reading my medical records.

I was put in a wheelchair and taken across the skywalk from the physician's office tower to the hospital. I was admitted, taken to triage, had an IV started, and put on the hospital gown. Then I was taken to a labor and delivery room. My nurse gave the introduction of what all she was ordered to do to me. She then hooked me up to every piece of machinery in the room. I had a BP cuff, fetal monitor, contraction monitor, heart and respiration monitor, catheter, and IV fluids and magnesium sulfate. I was given an injection of steroids to speed my daughter's development. The injection started the clock ticking on the 48 hours that my doctor wanted to give the steroids to take effect. As it turns out, 48 hours until delivery was a goal, but my condition dictated that time be abbreviated to 24 hours.

After this flurry of activity, my BP was becoming more alarming. The nurse would occasionally check my reflexes (you know the little rubber hammer to the knee routine?) Always, I had exaggerated reflexes. This troubled the nurse. For some reason, I found this funny. In my mind, the hammer to the knee was a silly thing that doctors did as rote during a routine physical, and no one ever knows why, and no one ever cares enough to ask because it's fun to watch. I had no idea why it was of such importance, especially since my reflexes seemed to be super sharp. That was good, right? I wanted to be given credit for passing at least ONE test thus far. But I was actually failing. More is not always better.

My husband and I understood very little about what was really going on at the time. Even though the specific test results were told to us, we didn't know what they meant. I know now that I was not given all of the information in order to prevent adding stress. The monitors were turned away from me, the shades are drawn, the temperature lowered, the TV turned off, and my husband was encouraged not to talk to me.

For all intents and purposes, the magnesium sulfate I was receiving put my body in a sort of suspended animation, and the rest of the measures were to deprive me of all stimulation in order to keep my BP from rising and causing seizures, stroke, and/or a coma. I tried to sleep to escape the severe headache and unbelievably bad heartburn, but I couldn't. My head felt like the top was going to blow off any minute. I retreated into nothingness. I felt as though I was in a long, dark tunnel with no exit. I prayed. I pleaded with God that if someone had to die, let it be me. I wanted the chance to raise my daughter; however, I knew that I could not live with my guilt or face my husband and my in-laws if my daughter did not live because of me. I knew that my life as I knew it was over and if my daughter did not live, and at the same time, I did live, that it would be Hell on earth. To use a gambling phrase, I went "all in" in my conversations with God.

As my condition worsened, I lost track of time. The pain in my head could not worsen. If I had known that a coma was the next feared step of my disease, I would have prayed for it just to have the relief of unconsciousness. I didn't know if it was day or night, and I began to wonder if I wasn't already dead. I did not know at this point that everyone had been asked not to talk to me. I thought that either I was already dead, and they were just keeping me hooked up to machines until they could deliver my baby or that they knew that death was imminent and was waiting for me to die. Despite the pain in my head and the thoughts of death, I had a very odd sense of calm. I knew that I had no control over the situation; that knowledge was a small comfort. At some point, I was somehow able to ignore the pain in my head. I hoped that if I was dead that they would discover my body and move it before it began to smell and rot.

Releasing my hold
To sink into depths untold
Anxiety rising fresh
To strike me stiff with stress

Thoughts of another
Take me places I can't discover
What the hell has past?
Random circumstance - relapse

Hurling through
What time? What place? What self?
Driven into
No clues to find, no help
Can't control you
When one becomes two ....

[Excerpt from lyrics of song,
One Becomes Two, by Forced Entry]

Then it was time to deliver the baby. Twenty-four hours had passed since I was admitted and received the first steroid shot, but it felt like a week to me. People were talking to me. Lights were on in the room. I was relieved that I had made it as long as I did in the tunnel, but I was worried that it was too soon to deliver the baby. I asked if they couldn't just keep me on the magnesium sulfate and let more time pass for my daughter's sake. I would willingly go back to the tunnel. My doctor said that no, we had to deliver the baby now. Delivery was the cure.

I'm told that my mother and brothers arrived and were allowed to visit with me. A couple of my friends were allowed in as well, but I don't remember. My father had not been able to get a flight from where he was teaching that week. I know he wanted to be there and was very upset that it couldn't be done. But as I told other friends later who weren't able to come to the hospital, it's okay. I wasn't allowed visitors, and I honestly don't remember. I remember that the clergy were always allowed. This was a new experience for me. Volunteer pastors from my church, most of whom I had never met, came to visit and pray for me. I've never been one to crave attention, but I really appreciated this. I was doing some serious praying, and I welcomed the help. They were so kind and always included me and my health in their prayers. I was always surprised and extremely grateful. I know that it helped.

My husband was worried about the epidural. I had my back to the nurse administering it, obviously. His eyes got as big as saucers, and he said, "Don't move, okay?" I sort of laughed and said, "I know." I had not seen the needle, and I was beyond worrying. I could not imagine the pain in my head getting worse; I was at the "10" on the stupid pain scale, so bring it on. I had decided that anything was worth it if it increased my daughter's chances; I didn't want to live unless she did too.

The epidural was given without incident, but it didn't work properly. My doctor described it as "spotty". I didn't have spots, but only portions of my body were numb. I got myself on the operating table to the astonishment of the staff assembled. Speaking of the operating room, it was not at all like those you see on TV. I was not happy to see that the operating table resembled a cross, to which the team planned to strap my arms. Indeed, I was laid prostrate before God and the team of medical professionals. However, willingly I had entered the room, however cavalier my attitude only a few minutes ago, now I wanted to go back to the nothingness of the tunnel. My arms were strapped to the cross. I was draped, and my doctor began to poke around on my belly. To the frustration of the anesthesiologist, I could feel the doctor's pinpricks on my belly. I had intended to endure anything, but I really didn't want to go through this operation without the benefit of the epidural. We all have our limits, and I had found mine. Prostrate or not, cross or not, ready for death or not, I was still conscious. Death and suffering are two different things. I didn't want to be awake to feel like they were cutting me to open. It was the one time throughout this entire process that I spoke up for myself. I have no idea why I didn't just faint.

Meanwhile, my husband was waiting patiently in my room, all dressed and ready to attend the birth of his child. This was going to be the good part! And this was the cure for the problem at hand. Five, ten, fifteen minutes passed, and he worried that they had forgotten to come to get him. While the anesthesiologist worked on me, my doctor left the sterile operating room to go tell my husband what was happening. After much ado, 40 minutes late, we were ready to begin the operation with my husband in the room. Even though I could only see his eyes, I could tell he was worried. My daughter was delivered while I was feeling much more of what was going on than I wanted. It was not paining like my headache, but I could feel it. I struggled to lie still, and at one point, I kicked the instrument tray. I begged them to hurry up and get finished. Finally, the tugging and pulling on my insides ceased, and they held up my daughter to let me see her before they took her away to the NICU. Her face was so tiny and cute, all bundled up like a burrito!

My husband stayed with me in the operating room, which he had planned to do, even though I really didn't expect him to once he saw our baby. But he did, and it meant a lot to me that he stayed with me. Then I was given general anesthesia, and mercifully the pain in my head and the knowledge of what was happening to my body behind the drape that I had been trying to ignore ended.

When I awoke, I was very disappointed to find that I was still receiving the magnesium sulfate. I wanted something to drink, and I wanted to be able to take something for the heartburn! I didn't feel that much different except for the worst of the headache had subsided. The doctor had added morphine to my IV as well as BP medication since the surgery to deliver my daughter. Pain is difficult to quantify even when you are experiencing it, and morphine plays tricks on your memory. Whether the narcotics blocked the memory of the past day or it was simply my mind in denial, I wasn't thinking about pain. My vision was still impaired. I had grown accustomed to the constant movement in my womb, and now it was gone. I felt a little lonesome. But the morphine made me more tolerant, and I was relieved at the reports that my daughter was doing well. The experience of the surgery was a distant memory even though it happened only about an hour or so before. The doctor told me that I had to be on the magnesium sulfate and morphine for 12 hours. Most people remember the narcotics fondly. And while I'm certain that they were preventing a bad experience, they weren't exactly pleasant for me. The darkness of the tunnel was "swirly". Even when I closed my eyes, the swirls of darkness were there. I didn't know if I was awake or asleep. It seemed as though time was standing still. Again I wondered if I was alive or dead with an odd sense of calm.

Behind The Mirror

As the fog lifted and light crept back into the room, I assumed that I was on the road to recovery. In fact, I was being coaxed through the steps that lead to discharge from the hospital. After a time, I was taken off of the magnesium sulfate and morphine. I was disconnected from all of the machinery and given a liquid dinner of beef broth, tea, and Jell-O. After my recent experience, this liquid dinner from the cafeteria was ambrosia! I was taken to the bathroom for the first time in 3 days. I was moved to a room in the post-partum ward. (For those that don't know, the post-partum ward is more like a hotel room than a hospital room. I was there for observation for the minimum amount of time with minimum staff before being discharged.) I was very tired from the move and was ready to try and savor what I figured was my last good night of sleep for a year or so. But the evening rounds of technicians still had to come by and take all my vital signs for the record.

I distinctly remember that the technician that hooked me up to the automatic machine and took my BP thought her machine was broken. She had never seen a reading that high, so she thought that it must be an error. The RN kept sending her back into my room with different BP machines, all with the same result. Then the RN told the technician that she must be doing something wrong. The technician was very frustrated. She very deliberately went through every step of putting the cuff on my arm, stepping away from me, and pushing the button to start the machine. It went through the now very familiar cycle of inflating and deflating. It was still a very high reading. So, finally, the RN took my BP the old-fashioned way-with a manual cuff and stethoscope. Yep, the same unusual reading—she finally had to believe that my BP really was that high. Since it was 11 pm at that point, the RN really did not want to call the doctor, but she did anyway. My OB/GYN gave orders that I be seen by the Maternal-Fetal Medicine Group during rounds the next morning (in 5 or 6 hours).

The next morning when I saw the doctor, the day I was to be discharged, my BP was high but not scary; the Maternal-Fetal Medicine doctor ordered that blood be drawn for other tests. The phlebotomist had a hard time finding me because it was unusual for her to be sent to the postpartum ward. The doctor also ordered that my BP be taken again in a few hours. But I was still on my way to being discharged. My husband and I trusted the doctors and what they were saying was consistent with what we had been told about the progression of the disease.

The 12 hour-shift of hospital personnel changed at 7 am. The newly assigned RN took my BP as ordered, not the technician. It so happened that my friends were visiting me at the time. The nurse seemed alarmed at the reading. She asked that my friends wrap up their visit while she reported the results to the doctor. The nurse came back a few minutes later, to take another reading. It was still high; apparently, it was scary. The nurse that took it had the same look on her face that the nurse in my doctor's office had when this all started. They looked at me as though I was a bomb about to go off. I remember my husband had begun to protest because things were not going as planned, but he quickly backed down when I suggested that he should look at the nurse's expression and that perhaps we should listen to the medical professionals. As soon as I sat down in the wheelchair, the RN was off, taking me back to the labor and delivery ward. She left me in the labor and delivery ward with an RN and gave her no choice but to keep me. Everyone was confused, but there I was. I couldn't go anywhere even if I had a mind to, as I was still mostly blind, could barely walk to the bathroom and back, had no idea where the exit was, or where my shoes and purse were for that matter. In hindsight, if not for that spike in BP and that RN forcing me back into a different ward, I would have been sent home just like Joan, the woman in "The Silence is Deafening". I am incredibly fortunate.

After being re-deposited in the labor and delivery ward while I was not in labor, and had already gone through delivery, the staff didn't know what to do with me, understandably. You see, in any hospital, there are definitely planned progression of events dictated by nature, hospital administrators, and health insurance companies that are and were expected to happen, and here I was going against the traffic. After much scurrying around, calling my doctor, consulting my chart for the events of last night, they put me in a room, started a new IV, hooked me up to every monitor that I had prior to delivery with the exception of the fetal monitor, gave me BP medication, deprived me of as many stimuli as possible, and watched me. The hope was that as the hours past after delivering the baby, my body would eventually "catch up to the program of expected events" and return to normal.

Meanwhile, I was told that my daughter was doing as well as possible down the hall in the NICU. My husband was trying to keep track of both of our needs. He did an outstanding job, by the way. As was apparent later, he remembered the result of every test and every entry into both my and our daughter's charts. He never missed an opportunity to quiz the nurses about what things meant and what was going on. He made sure that every order from the doctor was carried out and that all information was distributed to the nervous group of friends and family that had returned to the waiting room. And thankfully, they made sure that his basic needs were met as well. They brought food, clothes, the phone charger, and took care of our home and pets. Somehow, my mother, father, and siblings were picked up from the airport and brought to the hospital. I'm sure that we never thanked everyone enough, but I am grateful to everyone who was there to support my husband as he dealt with the flood of information and stress. Normally, he and I are partners in everything. But at this point, I now know that he had been told that both our daughter and his wife were in very serious condition and he should prepare himself for the possibility that he may lose us both. I wasn't any help. I was in a fog. I was being shielded from information to avoid any stimulus that would raise my BP. I don't know if it was the drugs being pumped into me or my mind retreating into the nothingness of the tunnel once again, but I was extremely worried about my daughter even though I was told she was doing well, and I just couldn't get my mind around what was happening to me. I prayed again for God to take me, not my daughter.

When anyone is under a lot of stress, they don't always react as expected or appropriately. I was withdrawn and silent. I think that my nurses and the nurses for my daughter were very worried about my reaction. In addition, I learned later that the waiting room of our family and friends were under a lot of stress and reacting to the news of the worsening conditions of me and my daughter, and to each other. While everyone can and is happy at the birth of a child, this particular birth has caveats. It wasn't typical; the joy of life was being closely pursued by death, and all that comes with it. For the group in the waiting room, the emotions were as thick, heavy, and conflicting as mine were. My husband and the hospital staff had to deal with caring for me and my daughter, as well as the small mob of very worried, emotional people that were showing signs of fracturing in the waiting room. We as a society are so fortunate to have the expectation that for every problem, there is a solution. When it became apparent that this birth was not going as planned, the fear and stress mounted.

My husband asked about pumping breast milk because the NICU was asking about it. We had always planned for me to breastfeed, but with all that had happened and given my current condition, my nurses were skeptical of the value of pumping and the added strain it would put on my system. Oddly, I really wanted to do it. If it was something that would be helpful to my daughter's health, I wanted to do it. So, the equipment was brought in, and a lactation nurse gave us our instructions. Because of the IV and all the monitors that I was attached to, my impaired sight, and my weakened state, I couldn't operate the pump. My husband had to do everything. But he did with great efficiency (he had worked on a dairy farm before, and as he pointed out, there wasn't much difference).

Now, before you get upset at my husband for being insensitive, this was a time where we giggled like adolescents - a welcome variation in mood. His observation was the truth. And honestly, I had the thought many times throughout pregnancy that it brought to the forefront of our conscious thought, bodily functions that which most people go to great effort to conceal or at least forget to happen on a daily basis. If I had thought pregnancy a vulgar experience, being hooked up to yet another machine that would pump milk from my breasts was over the top! And what girl likes being compared to a cow? Not one of them! I don't care how much you may welcome the joys of motherhood, cow comparisons are not fun, but sometimes you just have to laugh and get over yourself.

I was astonished, but my milk came in, and the pumping of breast milk went exactly as the lactation nurse said it would. It was good for both my husband and me to feel like we were doing something right! My friends later laughed that my husband kept referring to the process as "harvesting the milk" (as I said, he had worked on a dairy farm before). In any case, something was going well for me, and that was a bright spot in my experience.

However, my health did not return to normal, as was hoped.

Later the same day, I was moved to the antepartum (before delivery) ward. The labor room that I was in was needed for a person who was in labor. Again, I was going against traffic. It was apparent that no one really knew what to do with me or, more importantly, why my BP was not coming down to a normal level. I did not like being the source of such frustration. But once again, I knew that I had no control over the situation, and again, I had an odd sense of calm. I was hooked up to all of the machinery again with the exception of the catheter. I was on a 2-hour pumping schedule.

During the move, since I had to be removed from the machines anyway, I was taken to the NICU to see my daughter. I was afraid and excited. I put on my robe and rode in a wheelchair to the NICU. I was surprised at the security measures in place. We had to be buzzed in, but it was apparent that everyone knew my husband and was expecting us. It was difficult for me to scrub my hands and arms as instructed because of the IV ports still attached to me. It was all new to me, and I didn't understand it, but I was totally willing to do whatever was instructed. The NICU was small, hot, and crowded. Little Isolettes were parked in neat semi-circles according to needs. I strained to see into the Isolettes; I wanted to see all of the babies. My husband explained that everyone is asked to go directly to their baby's Isolette and not wander for privacy reasons. Despite the brightly decorated name tags and cheerful colors, and signs posted, each baby was in intensive care, and some were not going to live. The thick mixture of strong emotions in the room was palpable.

The nurses welcomed me in and explained everything. I was overwhelmed because this was the first time the gravity of my daughter's situation was made known to me. I was taught how to put my hands on my daughter's head and chest and to avoid stroking or light touches as her nerves were super sensitive, and constant touch was much more tolerable to her than light brushes. She looked perfect to me. My husband had described her to me and shown me a picture or two, but pictures never really give you a true perspective. She was incredibly tiny and looked different than most newborns because she was skinny. Her head was about the size of a baseball. My hand covered her entire torso. She stayed stretched out with her little limbs moving in jerky, uncoordinated movements. Up until that point, I had not asked about her much. I was afraid, and I had grown accustomed to the lack of interaction and information that my sensory deprivation, blindness, isolation, and exhaustion had brought on. But now that I had a glimpse of her, I wanted to know more, and my husband told me everything he had learned up until that point. I began to feel a little more like a partner again, even though; clearly, he was pulling most of the weight.

We couldn't stay long in the NICU; my nurses had said that I could not be away from the monitors for more than 30 minutes. Besides, it was hard for my daughter to have a lot of stimulation. I was hooked up in the antepartum room just as I had been in the labor and delivery room. I received my third IV in 5 days. Thankfully, because the surgery of the delivery was complete, they didn't use the really big needle for the second and third IVs, and instead of a 6 port apparatus, it was a much smaller 3 port apparatus. My hands and arms looked like a bruised pin cushion. My right arm wore the BP cuff that automatically inflated and took a reading every 15 minutes. It was a disposable cuff, and the hard plastic edges were making scrapes on my arm. The nurses and phlebotomists apologized profusely, but I understood the necessity of it all. These discomforts were nothing compared to the emotional toll. I can't say enough how much of an impression the nurses made on me. When I was my most wretched, and the doctors were making tracks out of the room, the nurses would run to my side to my aid and comfort. Nursing is not a job; it's a calling.

I was no longer receiving magnesium sulfate or morphine. My vision was still very limited to the peripheral. I slept a lot, that is, for the short periods of time when I wasn't pumping breast milk.

I was tired. I had been lying in a bed for three and a half days, but I was exhausted. I was tired of being sick. I was very frustrated with that stupid pain scale! After the headache I had endured, it was hard to measure pain from my surgery, especially since I was usually awoken from deep sleep to inquire what my pain was. Most of the time, I didn't feel I needed the pain medication. However, when my BP readings continued to go up and down erratically, one of the doctors said that pain could increase my BP, which may account for the spikes so that I should take the pain medication whenever it was offered. I spoke up and suggested that the doctor write the orders in a way that it is not offered as an option but as mandatory on a regular basis the appearance of reluctance to dispense it! Quit asking me to rate my pain! Compared to the last few days, my incision from the Caesarian was not painful.

In hindsight, the doctors were searching for any obscure reason why my BP was not coming down. They were as frustrated as I was. No one knew what to do. The medication I had been given was increased to its highest suggested dose over this period of time since the delivery, and it was not controlling my BP. My doctor declared me an enigma. She was right! So, after another day of the same, my doctor requested that two "hospitalists" be asked for an opinion. These doctors were accustomed to dealing with runaway BP in elderly patients. One of the doctors, while explaining what he was suggesting, actually said comparatively, I wasn't all that sick and that my BP was not the highest he had ever seen, but that in a person my age, it was unusual. The competitive side of me wanted to tell him that my test results were the highest my doctor had seen to date, and I had been in the hospital for 6 days, so somebody must believe me to be sick! But I refrained because, quite frankly, his diagnosis was preferable. I didn't want to be sick anymore. He suggested a cocktail of three separate very powerful drugs, in addition to the one I had been taking. The doctors apologized for giving me so many drugs, but I again found myself at the cavalier, it-can't-get-any-worse-than-this, "bring it on" stage.

Sometimes when I was first put into the antepartum wardroom, my father arrived. He was very upset that he was so late. But he came bearing a gift. He had brought me a teddy bear. He said that I was "his baby," and he really wanted me to know that. It was a very powerful, tangible gift. I knew my family and friends loved me and wanted me to get better. But after a week of offering my life up as a sacrifice to God for my daughter's, the teddy bear was a much needed and timely confirmation of my worth. I took the bear and kept him with me in my bed. I still have him.

I was given these "heavy-duty" drugs, but because they were typically given to geriatric patients, they either were not recommended for use in women who are breastfeeding, or they had not been tested at all. So, upon the advice of my OB/GYN, we had to dump two days worth of precious breast milk. Everyone who has ever nursed knows how much we hated to do this. Fortunately, I was already pumping far more than my daughter could consume, so the pain of watching the milk being dumped out was softened a little.

The other hospitalist that consulted on my case examined me and was especially interested in my reflexes. She felt my legs and closely examined my ankles. She said that she believed that I had too much fluid built up in my tissues. She prescribed a high dose of diuretic to help my body flush them out.

She was right! 50mg of HCTZ every 6 hours was the key to controlling my BP. While everyone had thought that I looked normal for a pregnant and post-partum woman at 30 weeks, I proceeded to lose

24 pounds of fluid in three days. Let me say that again; I lost 24 pounds in three days. I knew I was swollen! So, for three days, I peed, and peed, and sweated and sweated. My long hair, hospital gown, sheets, everything was wet from sweat. I was an amazing, shrinking woman. The change was dramatic. The heavy-duty drugs were able to work now that my heart was under less stress from fluid retention. My reflexes calmed as I shrunk. I was moved from the antepartum ward to the post-partum ward without passing through the labor and delivery ward. Again, I was going against traffic. But this time, there was much less confusion. My drugs were able to be adjusted to those that were safe for use while breastfeeding. The hospitalists came by to check on me and were very pleased with their work, as was I. My OB/GYN was very happy and relieved. The doctors seemed worried and hated to send me home with a bunch of prescriptions considering the work and years that I had ahead of me. One commented that if he looked in my pillbox, he would swear that I was a 70-year-old man, not a 35-year-old woman, post-partum. I swore to him that I would take the pills dutifully and without complaint if that was what was warranted.

The counselor from the NICU came to visit me. She was very worried about me, post-partum depression, and what I had ahead of me. Her relief was apparent through my improving but still blurry vision when I assured her that I already had a counselor and would most definitely be contacting her. And I also assured her that at this point, I had no objection to an anti-depressant and would take whatever drug was warranted for my condition. (A side effect of hypertension and any heart problem is depression. And post-partum is always a concern for new mothers.)

After a brief rest at home, as much sleep as I could get while pumping every two hours, I went back to work. My daughter was still in the NICU. While I could have begun my maternity leave and used my time to stay with my daughter in the NICU, I decided that it was better to conserve my leave time for when she could come home. The nurses assured me that there was really nothing that I could do but to continue to deliver the breast milk and make short visits when I could. I went back to work for 6 hours each day. I got up at 5:30 am, and my mother had breakfast ready, and my lunch packed. I pumped at 6 am, left the house by 6:30 am. I arrived at the office at 7 am, worked 6 hours straight while taking two breaks to pump. I left work at 2 pm and went straight to the hospital with my tiny cooler of breast milk. I visited my daughter for 30 minutes, used their lactation room to pump again, then headed home. My mother had dinner ready for me. I ate, then changed out of my working clothes and went straight to bed for an hour. My husband came home, ate dinner with my parents, then woke me up.

I pumped, and we headed to the NICU. Each night, after the night shift nurses arrived, families came in and took care of their babies, usually from 7:30 pm to 8:30 or 9:00 pm. After scrubbing up like a surgeon and donning a hospital gown over our clothes, parents got to hold their babies for a total of 20 minutes; the babies were fed & weighed, and every fraction of an ounce gained was cause for celebration. Then the babies were given their bath, and sensors changed. Then when they were all taken care of, they were put in their isolettes to go to sleep. The whole process took a little over an hour. Then we drove home, I pumped again, collapsed into bed for a couple of hours, got up pumped, slept a couple of hours, pumped, and it was time to start the whole thing over again.

We kept up this schedule for 5 more weeks. Finally, we got the good news. We were going home with our baby! I was so happy but terrified at the same time. For the last 6 weeks, my daughter had teams of trained professionals and wonders of technology watching over her every minute of every day. I felt completely unqualified. But the thought of getting to hold her anytime I wanted for as long as I wanted was quite an incentive.

Once we got home, I spent the next 12 weeks holding my baby as much as possible. Many hours were spent in an antique oak rocking chair that had been used by young and old in my family for generations. It squeaked and creaked, and it was incredibly comfortable. My daughter and I seemed most happy in the noisy chair together. We savored every minute. I am so thankful!

After a few weeks, I did not need the "heavy-duty" drugs. Unfortunately, five years later, I still have high BP, and my body retains fluid. I take pills every day though a drastically reduced number of pills. In fact, I take the same pills that my dad takes. I don't like taking them, and I don't like the side effects, but it is better than the alternative. The good thing is that "Hypertension", as is now my diagnosis has many drugs available to control it. Once I was finished breastfeeding, my drug options were expanded, and I have found a combination that works well for me. God answered my prayer. We both lived through it.

My daughter is now 5 years old and attending Kindergarten. I continue to see my counselor about this and anything else in life that bothers me. I wouldn't give it up for anything!

Post Script—I hope my story will help the medical industry to understand the need for a road less traveled' to be constructed. There was obviously, no plan for the path that my disease took. I could have easily been a statistic. I hope that my living to tell it and to put it on paper is a contribution to all those women who didn't live. I want to help make those statistics improve.

Post, Post Script - I know nothing of Forced Entry, a thrash metal band from Seattle, Washington. But their lyrics popped up when I Google-ed the phrase, "one becomes two". I was searching for thoughts and explanations of duality and the intense, conflicting thoughts and feelings that I am trying to convey in this story. Honestly, I've never heard the song as it was intended. But the lyrics are a perfect fit for my purpose. They are beautiful, raw, rough, and refined while describing something natural, base, gruesome, beautiful, selfless, selfish, divine, mysterious, dark, and evolving.

JOURNEY 9

Relationships can either be something good or -in my case- a bad thing with the 'wrong' person. Sixteen years ago, I met a man who I thought I loved and also loved me back. His love was different from my love; it consisted of putting his hands on me. I was a battered woman, verbally, and physically abused. I was raised in a really good, typical middle-class family where making a wrong choice attracted standard punishments. Having come from a loving family, I was not used to being abused or anything of such.

Yet, I lived with a man who was very jealous and controlling for 5 years. My friends were few and didn't come around because he was so mean. You never knew what would come out of his mouth at any time. He was so disrespectful, and I never spoke to any of my male friends and also advised them not to speak to me. We never had any date nights because I was too embarrassed to go anywhere with him. I never knew what would pop off if we went out on a date in public. Perhaps, you're curious and might want to ask how I ended up with someone like him in my life? The truth was that he wasn't anything like that when we first met. A woman's intuition kept telling me different, but I didn't listen. My first clue should have been the fact that he had no real solid relationship with his mother, and he didn't know his dad or make any conscious effort to. ALL RED FLAGS, ladies! Without guidance as a child, you will not know anything different than what you have been taught. These are signs that he will not know how to treat or love you. REMEMBER KIDS MIMIC WHAT THEY SEE!

If you think that you can change a man (my second mistake), it's not possible if he's not willing to change to a better person, and accordingly, the relationship doesn't have a chance. The results will stay the same. In the long run, he will change you to be just like him. I became a bitter, hateful woman. I became someone I didn't like at all. I hated to look in the mirror to the woman I had become.

It took the death of my mother to help me realize that it was time to go. When your man is not there to support you through your time of need, and you have no one else. He felt like helping me get through this tough time in my life would be a great time to get high on drugs. This was his idea of coping. I'd had enough!

One day, I stood in front of that mirror again and looked at myself. I said, who are you? I broke down. That moment right there, I prayed, told God that if he would get me out of this situation, I would never return again. I started going to church, bible study, and kept myself busy in the church. That's when I found my passion for spiritual dance. I could tell my story through dancing, and that became my ministry.

Months went by until God said, "go find yourself a place to live and put your trust in me." I found myself a brand-new apartment that had never been lived in and was exactly what I could afford. This is how God works. I had the money for the deposit but didn't think I would have enough for the 1st-month rent. I signed the lease for the apartment, went home, and checked the mailbox. A child support check for the amount I needed and even had extra leftover for me to turn my lights on at the new apartment. I knew that there was nothing that God couldn't do. I packed my stuff and told my girls we were leaving. I left clothes and a lot of stuff that I purchased right there. I left all of those things behind. I didn't want any reminders of that relationship.

The funny thing is that I actually told him it wasn't going to work, and the only thing I asked was that he took care of his responsibilities. He agreed, but let's not get it twisted, he tried to come back in my life with promises of change, but I couldn't go down that road again. The hardest part for me was to forgive. I struggled with the situation even today.

Let's fast forward to the present day. Through all that I've been through, I love the woman I have become. I'm a GOD fearing, praying, praising, can put a spiritual dance together at the drop of a dime. In more ways than one, I am blessed, and I hope that you're also blessed in even more ways than I've been. But just remember this…. TRY HIM ENOUGH TO TRUST HIM AND TRUST HIM ENOUGH TO TRY HIM. GOD IS A GOD THAT WILL NEVER LEAVE YOU OR FORSAKE YOU.

JOURNEY 10

My Journey starts around the late 1960's and 1970's; where I was called colored girl to black girl and now African-American. I remember mostly being called colored-girl. Like any childhood, I had some ups and downs. I am the youngest child of seven children (4 boys and 3 girls). I had an older sister who passed away at the age of three from 'Hydrocephalus' (which is an increase of fluid around the brain). This condition made my sister's head swell. My mother always told me never to call anyone big-head because of what her baby looked like when she passed away.

Being the youngest of seven kids, I was always seen as the little sister who had to be protected from the world. My family lived in an almost all-white neighborhood, which in the 1960's and 1970's was a hard thing for white people to accept. Our family was looked down on by not only the white race for being in the all-white neighborhood but the black race as well. We were treated as if we were on a lower level than our neighbors, even though we lived in the same kind of house as some of our neighbors. Many black people always told us we thought we were better than them because of where we lived. Neither of which was actually true. We always thought we were the same as everyone else. My father worked hard and was able to buy a house for us to live in, and never did it occur to us that we would be judged by both races, just simply because we lived in a neighborhood.

Since we lived in this neighborhood, we went to a predominately white school due to our district. When it was time for my first year at school, I was the only black in my class through 5th grade. Entering

6th grade, I met another black girl who is now my best friend. During the time at this school, I was called colored, dirty, and ugly. when I would get home in the afternoon the only thing that made me feel better was seeing my mother. My mother would always tell me, "Lisa, you are beautiful".

In the 1970's, we had to put up with a lot of racist people who taught their kids what they learned in the 1940's. In the beginning, I would be pushed to the back of the lunch line, picked last for games; I couldn't touch them because I was black. Most kids wanted to touch my hair because it was different, and the texture was different. Sometimes, my feelings would get hurt, and a couple of times, it would end in fights. I had to overcome the racist remarks and their actions. I decided to make the best of the situation and played with the few little girls who didn't mind hanging out with me on the playground.

Moving on to Junior high school seemed to get a little better. I was still very shy, and most people thought I was just being stuck up because I wouldn't talk to them or thought I was better than them. Even though it seemed to be a mixture of all races at Junior high school at times, I would still hear negative remarks.

When arriving at high school, I still was shy, but I felt better about my friends and grew closer to a lot of them from Jr. high school. Everything started to turn, and things begin to be fun. I started feeling my confidence build up and actually started feeling I was a pretty black girl.

While in high school, I lost my hearing in my left ear and some in my right ear. My parents took me to Fort Knox VA Hospital, where they ended up doing surgery on my ears. Since my father was a disabled Veteran, we always went to a VA Hospital. During my high school sophmore year I met my husband who was my friend at the time.

In my senior year, we were again introduced at Burger King, where I worked. I graduated high school in 1987 and married my sweetheart in July of 1987. In the summer, I recieved admission to Western Kentucky University in the fall semester and began my studies as a medical laboratory technician. I always knew that I was going to be in the medical field. My husband and I decided during my sophomore year of college to move to Nashville, TN. While living in Nashville, Tennessee, I earned my degree as a medical assistant. At this time, I felt that everything was going as planned until I found out the college had lost its accreditation, and I couldn't take any test to certify me as a medical assistant. Basically, I felt like I'd wasted a full year of time and money spent at a college that wouldn't help me earn a degree.

In 1989, I found out I was pregnant with our first child and soon gave birth to a wonderful baby boy named Jerrell Michaels Love. I found a job at the YMCA, where they sent me to schools to work with the after-school programs; this program was called the Fun Company.

So, things seemed to be going fine with our new son and job, but it all seemed to be falling apart at home. Our marriage was going through difficult times, but I still loved my husband. He was a good man and worked all the time just like a husband should, but I still missed that companionship. Instead of talking to my husband about the things I was feeling or at least seek help through a counselor, I didn't say anything. Everything was getting better when we started going to church together and getting involved in church programs. In 1995, we had a car accident on the way to get the kids, and I was taken to the hospital. The doctors did a scan of my head and found I had broken a bone in my ear and that I needed another surgery. This surgery fixed the right ear, but I have lost complete hearing in my left ear till today.

After the accident, we slowly stopped going to church, and when

God stepped out of our life, the devil stepped right in and made himself comfortable in our home again. I started eating more and gaining more weight. My husband started talking down on me about my weight gain and that I wasn't doing anything to correct my weight. Depression started to set in, and then one day, I had a seizure. The fall-out of the seizure saw me diagnosed with epilepsy. I was fat, depressed, and had seizures all the time.

After 20 years of ups and downs, we went our separate ways, and this time it was for good. My son moved with his father most of the time during his college years. From 2007 to 2012, it was just me and my daughter. Due to my seizures, I still had to find ways to get to work and take my daughter places. One day, while driving with about 5 children in the car, I had another seizure leading to another car crash. Due to the grace of God, there were no major injuries, and my daughter, and I only had bruises to show from a totaled Toyota Camry.

From this point on, I seemed to stay depressed, but I did find time to get involved by helping a church program for the youth. The program turned into a non-profit organization for the youth and young adults in the Tennessee area.

The work I was doing to help this organization also was helping me get stronger. In 2012, I decided to move back to Bowling Green, Kentucky, to help my father and mother since both of them have had health issues and needed more help around the house.

Day by day, it seemed to get better by working with the non-profit organization and also getting back in touch with my best friend. This is the same friend from 6th grade that had introduced me to some powerful, uplifting women in Bowling Green, Kentucky. I found a sisterhood of women that want to help others and, most of all, uplift and just be a true, good friend. I will always love these women, who helped me get through the storm that was raging in my life. These women taught me to love myself and, most importantly, God. If you don't love yourself, then no one else will love you. You must remember how important you are and start by loving yourself.

Now I am no longer that dirty, little, colored-girl or fat, ugly, black girl. I know that I am a strong, beautiful African-American woman who will let no man or woman tear her down again. Like everyone, I still have bad days, but I always look to my hospice patients who I take care of on a daily basis. Being their nursing assistant has clearly opened my eyes that my day is not that bad, after all. I am a child of God, and I will stay positive. I learned through those 20 years of marriage; the best time was when we had God in our life. I learned in a marriage, you put God first and then your spouse. I believe if the word of God is not in your heart, it can lead your marriage into a bad situation.

I decided to let God lead while I followed. Now, after 4 years, I've been seizure-free.

JOURNEY 11

I am a native of Warren County. I am single, 57-years old, presently working at the Bowling Green Human Rights Commission. I hold two title positions, 'Administrative Coordinator' and 'Fair Housing Outreach Education Coordinator'. My responsibilities are very detailed such as assisting clients with complaints in discrimination in Employment, Housing, and Public Accommodation under the protected classes regardless of race, color, sex (meaning gender), age (over forty), disability, national origin, familial status, and religion. I assist clients not just with complaints but other situations and circumstances when they don't know who to ask for assistance. Our office provides a resource community listing of referrals to other agencies and organizations that might provide services to help throughout our community of Bowling Green and Warren county. I requisition supplies that are needed in the office, correspond with city and county government officials and twelve board of commissioners through e-mail of board minutes, financial reports, events, activities and etc. I attend meetings with our community partners, such as the Homeless and Housing Coalition of South Central Kentucky and the purpose of our coalition is to assist the homeless. It's in the process of organizing the "Room in the Inn" for homeless individuals through church congregations. Our office conducts fair housing workshops for property managers, landlords, various agencies, businesses, and community partners. Our agency goes out in the community, participates, and attends banquets, ribbon-cutting ceremonies, events, workshops, open houses, and various activities.

What I love most about my job position is that I've had an opportunity to interact, meet, assist, and educate the public about issues they're not aware of and who could assist them with their situations.

In August of 1998, I lost my job at Trans Financial Bank after eleven years of service. First Star Bank bought out Trans Financial Bank, and my position was no longer needed because it was transitioned to Ohio. I had an opportunity to go to Western Kentucky University for 2 years of school paid in full through the dislocated worker program. I received my vacation pay, severance pay, collected my unemployment, and I got paid $10.00 per day to attend school, and also, I received my retirement pay. I didn't have to work for one whole year; thanks be to God. I received my Associate's Degree in Management of Information Systems with emphases of Business Technology. While attending college and being a full-time single mother caring for my two sons and also during that time, my mother became ill, and I had to take care of her. I had a lot on me for my first semester taking 15 hours of college courses, plus cooking, cleaning, transporting my mom back and forth to the doctor, paying the bills, grocery shopping, helping my sons with homework, and including squeeze homework time and studying time into my busy schedule. When I look back over my life during that time, I won't complain because I know things could have been worse, and I know I wouldn't have made it without the Lord on my side because he gave me the strength to endure.

I have a couple of aspirations I'd like to accomplish, such as completing my Bachelor's Degree in Business Administration /General Management, in which I only need one year. My second thing is waiting on the Lord to see what else he has for me to do in my life!! I have two handsome sons, and their names are Asa Ke'Amethyst Sparks and Khalin Breuon Sparks.

My healthy lifestyle includes exercising, cardio, weight lifting, and

Zumba on Tuesdays and Thursdays from 5:30-6:30 p.m. at Bowling Green Parks and Recreation Center. I am very well pleased with my healthy lifestyle.

I would love to change my eating habits by eating less bread and rolls and begin walking outside when the weather cools down.

When I began this weight-loss journey, my goal was to lose 50 pounds; so far, I have accomplished my goal by losing half 28 pounds.

I am continuing and dedicated to my health program, such as portion control, no sodas, limited myself to just drinking water and crystal-lite, eat plenty of salads, nuts, vegetables, fruits, baked, and grilled foods such as fish and chicken, and a very limited amount of sweets. My limited intake of sweets includes slim fast bars, granola bars, and fat-free ice cream.

This chapter of my life began with my past-illness, a life-changing event that'd occurred. I was diagnosed with breast cancer on Friday, February 19, 2010, at 2:00 p.m. at the Medical Center. I went to my dr. appointment alone to have my annual mammogram. The nurse detected a lump in my left breast. I had to have an ultrasound on my left breast by a radiologist. When I left the hospital, I was very up-set because of the disturbing news. I called my mother, Mrs. Reddie Sparks, and Mrs. Linda McCray, Executive Director of the Bowling Green Human Rights Commission, to tell them what they said about my mammogram.

I went to see my mother and my son Asa tell them the news. By now, my breast had begun to hurt, and I couldn't tell exactly where it was hurting, but it hurt because the mammogram had disturbed it. The following Monday, February 22, 2010, at 3:00 p.m. My mother, Linda, and I went with me to see my gynecologist. He explained that

I had a category 6 tumor, which means the size of the tumor, and it was located at 12:00, which also means the location of the tumor. In the back of my mind, I was thinking, could it be cancer? I asked the doctor, "Is it possible that it could be cancer?" He said, "Generally, cancer doesn't hurt." Then I went on to tell him that this does hurt. He said it could be benign, which means it couldn't be cancer. That's why he's referring me to a surgeon. When I came out of the doctor's office, my sister, Ti'Sha, was waiting for me to come out of the office. I was indescribably upset because I knew I had to have surgery. I also knew where it was and how big it was, but I just didn't know what it was at the time. Before I went to see the surgeon, I had to go back to the hospital to pick up my films and DVD of my left breast. The doctor referred me to a surgeon the very next day on Tuesday, February 23, 2010, at 1:15 p.m. I, my mother, and Linda go to see the surgeon. In saying, before the doctor, examined my breast, he asked me to do you mind if he could have a prayer? I told him, "I don't mind. I need all the prayers I can get." When he prayed, it gave me confirmation about this surgeon; he wasn't relying on science and medicine, but he was relying on God to do what he needed to do for me as his patient. The doctor performed another ultrasound scan on my left breast; he then suggested that I had to have a biopsy. This is what he said to me, "I generally don't do biopsies on Thursday, but I'm going to work you in because I am concerned about the lump." That should have been a sign to me, but it didn't register on me quickly enough how serious the tumor was at that particular time. Here I was again, upset and in tears because I didn't know what to expect. The doctor made my appointment for Thursday, February 25, 2010, at 11:30 a.m. I had my biopsy procedure, which was to vacuum out the tissue from the tumor. I was in so much pain afterwards. My Mom and Linda took care of me, and my cousins Fonnie and Helen came to see about me. The doctor said I should have my results by next Tuesday, March 01, 2010. His nurse told me to give them a call before we come to make sure my results were there. I called the office on Tuesday to find out if the results were there, and they were. So, I, along with mom and Linda, go back to the doctor's office to find out what the tumor was. The news was malignancy (CANCER). The tears flowed freely because the first thought we had was that, "I'm going to DIE." The word cancer has a lot of emotions attached to it. I didn't know what stage it was or anything. The doctor left out of the waiting room so we could collect our thoughts. He came back in and handed me a book to read. He had marked certain pages for me to read overdue to the surgery. The doctor said that I had 2 options; I could have a lumpectomy, which means just to remove the lump only, or a mastectomy, which means to remove the entire breast. The doctor told me that he could perform my surgery on Thursday, and I said, "This Thursday?" "He said yes." I told Dr., let me talk to my sons about my situation before I make a decision about anything. "He said," ok, we'll need to see you back here tomorrow, which was on Tuesday, March 02, 2010, at 3:45 p.m. to schedule my surgery. I was extremely upset at this time because I knew I had cancer, I had to have surgery, and I only had the 2 options. I had so much information thrown at me so fast I didn't have time to comprehend it all. It was hard for me to process it all mentally and emotionally. I understood that I had a window to go by in order for the doctors to treat cancer that I had so it wouldn't spread throughout my body. My two sons Asa and Khalin, knew that I had a doctor's appointment to see what the results were from the biopsy. Linda drove me and mom back home; Asa and Khalin were there waiting on us. I sat down with them and told them that it was CANCER. It had to register with them first before they could have any reactions to the news I had just told them. We all had our moments of crying for a while. Then Asa suggested that it's time for prayer, and then he said it's not real until it hits home, and I had to agree with him. So, we all stood in the middle of the floor, holding hands and crying as we PRAYED. My sister, Ti'Sha, came to pick me and my mom up to take us to the doctor's office to schedule my surgery for Thursday, March 04, 2010. We had a lot of questions for him to answer. Due to my current affliction of breast cancer at that particular time, I was mentally and emotionally distraught that Ti'Sha had the mindframe and took the initiative to ask the surgeon the questions while taking notes on each answer that were necessary for me to know.

My decision was to have a lumpectomy after talking it over with my family. Mom took me to Pre-op at Greenview Hospital on Wednesday, March 03, 2010, at 12:30. I had to have lab work done and x-rays. I couldn't eat or drink anything after 12:00 on Wednesday night before surgery on Thursday. My surgery was scheduled for 1:30 p.m. on Thursday, March 04, 2010. I remember some things about that day, such as; I had to be there at 9:30 a.m. Ti'Sha came to pick up mom and me about 9:00 a.m. The nurse came to get me about 9:35 a.m. to register me in a room with the IV in my hand. She took my blood pressure and temperature, put the hospital gown on me, asked me some questions such as my name, what's the reason I was there, and my birthdate. Then the nurse went to get my family and brought them into the room before surgery.

Due to the upcoming surgery, I was extremely nervous, and I must admit that I was a little scared. My sister Ti'Sha asked the nurse would she give me a sedative, and she did. I had another nurse to come and explain to me about the blue dye test they were going to do before my surgery. This test would show if I had any cancer in my lymph nodes. That test took about 2 hours, 11:00–1:00 p.m. I asked the nurse to let me see my family once again before I actually went into surgery. Well, they did; mom, my sons, Asa, Khalin, my sister, Ti'Sha, my cousin Fonnie, and cousin Helen were all there. I talked to them, and they hugged and kissed me before I went back to surgery. I can remember them rolling me back down the hall as I talked with the doctor. I had another nurse to ask me the exact same questions again, which were; my name, the reason I was there, and my birthdate. While she was asking me those questions, she was injecting the anesthesia into my IV. I remember them rolling me into the surgery room, and that's all. It seemed like my surgery took 5 minutes when I woke up. I was told it was 2 hours long. I remember a nurse asking me was I in pain, and all I remember was moaning and groaning, and she gave me 3 morphine shots and ice chips. When they rolled me back to the recovery room, only 2 people at the time could see me. I remember, Asa and Khalin were 1st, Fonnie and Linda were 2nd; they came in to feed me crackers and water. I also remember telling Fonnie and Linda that I saw a big baby with a little stripped shoe. They were laughing at me, but it seemed so real to me. It wasn't anything but the drugs talking. And I remember Mom, Fonnie, and Linda trying to get me dressed and trying to put my shoes on my feet, and they were not fitting my feet. I could hear the nurse talking, but I couldn't comprehend what she actually was saying. The nurse was explaining to them how to take care of me when they got me home after surgery.

At this point, I was so out of it from the anesthesia and morphine shots that I couldn't even stand up. They wheeled me to the car, and I remember it being dark outside. Linda drove me and my mom home, and Khalin helped walk me into the house. I thought I would never get to my bedroom. That was the longest drive-way I've ever walked in my life life. Lastly, but not at least I also remember Khalin feeding me crackers and soup, and that's all I remember until the next morning. The next morning when I woke up, I was so sore that I couldn't lay flat at all, I was swollen, and I hurt no matter which way I would move. I remember sitting straight up to sleep at night. I was in pain even though I was on hydrocodone and promethazine, and I slept all the time. I had to have help to get up from the chair, bed, bathe myself, clothe myself, and even use the bathroom. I couldn't drive, cook, or clean. I had my first appointment to see the doctor after my surgery on Thursday, March 11, 2010, 10:00 a.m. He took off the big patch and looked at my incision to see how it looked, and he also told me that my cancer was actually in stage 1. Therefore, he was going to refer me to a radiologist; and I was recommended to have Chemotherapy Treatments and Radiation Treatments.

My first appointment with the radiologist was Thursday, March 18, 2010, at 1:15 p.m. My second appointment with an oncologist was Monday, March 22, 2010, at 12:45 p.m. My treatments would begin with Chemotherapy; first treatment because my tumor was 3-cm large, which was the size of a ½ dollar, which threw my cancer into stage 2. I was recommended to undergo 4 treatments of Chemotherapy beginning on Wednesday, April 14, 2010, at 10:00 a.m. Chemotherapy treatments would be (1) treatment every 3 weeks. The doctor recommended thirty-three treatments of Radiation. My treatments would be for 5 ½ weeks beginning Wednesday, June 30, 2010, at 1:00 p.m. I would have to undergo radiation treatment every single day until it was completed. I have to say this, "I give GOD all the glory and the Praise for letting my illness be as well as it is/was because I know it could have been a lot worse." I had a wonderful support system; it's the best system you'll ever need when cancer strikes you, a friend, co-worker, or even a family member.

You'll need someone to go with you for each Dr. Visit to ask questions for you and even take notes for you because you can't think of things to ask because you are still processing the fact you have cancer. I cried, and I just couldn't help myself. When you hear the word "Cancer" spoken from a doctor's lips, it's heartbreaking; all you can think about is that I'm going to die. I actually was in denial for a long time because I didn't want to think I had cancer then. One day it came to me that I accepted the fact that I did indeed have cancer.

That's when I gave this battle of cancer to the Lord, and I said, "Lord, this battle isn't mine to fight; it belongs to you, so I gave it all to the Lord." Look at me now. I am still here!

I have two favorite scriptures: *Philippians 4:13 "I can do all things through Christ, which strengthens me."*

Psalm 30:5 "For his anger endureth but a moment; in his favour is life: weeping may endure for a night, but joy cometh in the morning."

You need as much support and words of encouragement as you can possibly receive on the other end of that phone, verbally and even through their Prayer!

This is very important; three things that were told to me

- Keep your Faith in GOD
- Keep a positive attitude
- Don't give up.

I have and will continue to pass this on to others fighting the battle of breast and other cancers. This is very important to be careful about how you treat others because you never know when you are going to need someone to do something for you!

I had so many blessings crossing my path from every direction south, north, east, and west of Bowling Green. They all came from the lord. I had sincere prayers sent up for me; I had meals prepared for me and sent to me, I had cards mailed and sent to me with financial support in them, I had items brought and sent to me, I had so many phone call blessings checking on me just to see how I was doing. I had gifts sent and brought it to me. I had visits from everybody coming to see about me. When I think of god's goodness, it makes me want to shout so bad.

One thing I can't wait to shout and tell my story of how I made it over by god's grace and mercy that brought me through it and kept me the entire time of my illness. This chapter of my life is a test of my faith and my faith in him, and I know god for myself. Nobody has to tell me about him because I know him for myself. I had to accept my illness and trust, lean, and depend on God for my illness, treatment, and cure, which was all in his hands. This battle was not mine to fight; it belonged to the lord to fight for me. I overcame my illness through god's blessings of family and friends near and far, and that's how I got through those tough days of having breast cancer. I kept a daily journal with every name, phone number, every card sent, every meal made, and every act of kindness that crossed my path that was poured out and worked through to become my blessings from my lord and Savior Jesus Christ.

There aren't enough words that can express how I and my family were truly blessed during this time of my illness. That's how I overcame my illness, and this is why I am a Breast Cancer Survivor,, my journey through Breast Cancer gave me a Testimony!

I am presently continuing to be monitored, and follow-up with appointments under the Doctors care until the year 2015 with medication. In saying I had my yearly mammogram on June 20, 2014, and I had some calcifications to show up on my mammogram, therefore, I was referred back to my surgeon for another biopsy on the same exact breast. I have to thank God for my wonderful support system. They are great, my mother (Mrs. Reddie Sparks and Mrs. Linda McCray). My biopsy was conducted on Monday, June 30, 2014; I did receive my results on Thursday, July 03, 2014, and did not have malignancy. I (Praise God) every time I have a chance for his goodness. My surgeon placed a flag inside my breast, so when I go back in 6 months for another mammogram, they will know that I've had a biopsy on that area.

I don't have any specific dreams at the moment, but I am trying to live my life to the fullest as I possibly can. There is a difference between living your life and just existing in life. I'm looking forward to becoming a wife and grandmother someday!

My inspirational advice is love; it is the greatest gift we have because "God is Love."

I, John 4:8, "He that loveth not knoweth God; God is love." I like to inspire anyone and everyone that crosses my path because you never know what that person(s) need at that moment. Sometimes you can inspire a person with a handshake, a hug, and even words of encouragement. It's not what you do for a person, but it's how you make them feel while being in your presence. Love others as you love yourself and treat others the way you want to be treated.

My spiritual advice is to develop a very personal and sincere relationship with Jesus Christ, our Savior.

Matthew 7:7-8 "Ask, and shall be given you; seek, and ye shall find; knock, and the door shall be opened unto you. For everyone that askethreceiveth; and he that seekethfindeth; and to him that knocketh it shall be opened."

In saying, I would suggest that you ask God to send you to a church, get involved in church activities such as Bible Study, Prayer Meetings, Sunday School, Worship, and Praise Services. You will learn how to live Godly lives and learn about our Savior Jesus Christ, who died for all of our sins. You will learn how to give thanks to him, pray every day, and ask God for guidance and direction in your life/lives.

You will learn how to lean and depend on God daily; also, ask God in Faith for whatever trial or tribulation that comes into your life/lives.

Matthew 17:20 "Because of unbelief: for verily I say unto you. If ye have faith as a grain of mustard seed, ye shall say unto this mountain, remove hence to yonder place, and it shall remove, and nothing shall be impossible unto you."

Therefore, you will have a true foundation with the Lord. Just because you can't see him doesn't mean he's not there because when you become a true believer, he is there all of the time.

2 Corinthians 6:14 "Be ye unequally yoked together with unbelievers for what fellowship hath righteousness with unrighteousness? And what communed hath light with darkness?"

If you are striving do date a person that is a worldly individual, and you are a believer in Christ Jesus, I can tell you it will not prosper into a healthy relationship. I am a witness not once but twice, and that is a true fact.

Ti'Sha, my dear sister, if you are reading my life journey, I just want you to know this.

I am so thankful and grateful to God for sending me a sister like Ti'Sha Loving-Williams. She is a wonderful woman that I truly love and adore. Ti'Sha is a bit younger than me, but we have one thing in common we both shared a wonderful brother that passed on about 22 years ago. Since then, Ti'Sha and I have grown as sisters down through the years, and for that, I am grateful. She is so special and lovely young lady. I thank God for her being a part of my life, and I couldn't imagine my life without her. Ti'Sha, I want to give you your flowers while you live so you can smell the beauty of them.

I want to thank you for allowing me to share my life journey in your project, and I know it will be a great success because you are the best. Ti'Sha, you are such a beautiful woman inside and out, and you are loved by many. I am your greatest fan and sister. In saying, "Ti'Sha, you are a wonderful wife and beautiful mother and a true friend to many that cross your path." In addition, Ti'Sha, you have gifts and accolades; she is an awesome event coordinator. On a much more personal note, I would like to express my sincere gratitude to Ti'Sha for sacrificing her time, effort, and energy in supporting me in the time of need while also taking care of her family and sacrificing her time from her full-time career. I pray that God will continue to shower you with all his blessings from above now, and always, I love you!!

I took great joy in writing down my life journey, and I wouldn't change it for anything because this is the life I've been dealt and how I live it and is what makes life worth living. I've had some wonderful life experiences and some good and some not so good. But that's just life, but I've come to realize in this life, all you truly need is the BIBLE (**B**asic **I**nstructions **B**efore **L**eaving **E**arth).

JOURNEY 12

I don't know where to begin. I guess I should start out with a moment in my life that I know forever changed me. I should take a moment to at least say I had a wonderful childhood with great parents... so not for one moment in my journey would I want you to think that my wild days are a reflection of my parent's "parenting skills". I was a wild teenager, and there wasn't much my parents could do except love me and try and guide me the best they could.

The moment in my life that forever changed me was my 14th birthday. On May 28th, 1998, in the middle of the night, I had the bright idea to sneak out in the middle of the night (as I had done several times in the past) and steal my parent's car. I went and picked up a friend, and we went for a long drive. Somehow, we ended up lost and scared. I remember there was this guy that started following us in his car, and we got super scared. I decided to speed up to try and lose him. I ended up going so fast around "dead man's curve" that the car went off the road and flipped about 15 times in a cornfield. Once the car came to a complete stop, I struggled to climb out of the totaled vehicle and pull my friend out too. We were standing in a cornfield, lost, scared, and didn't know what to do. We started walking until we found a house with their lights on. As we started walking to the house, my friend begged me not to call my parents. I knew I had no choice but to call them because we needed help. I knocked on a door at 2AM, and a man answered the door. I explained to him what happened, and he let me use his phone to call my parents. I remember trying to call them and kept getting a "can't complete your call as dialed". It turns out we were somewhere in Scottsville, and we had to call my parents long distance. My parents rushed to our location and took us straight to the ER. I was treated right away for my injuries, but my friend was not. The ER would not treat her without permission from her parents. My friend's parents were not answering their phone. They had to send a neighbor to their house to bang on the window until her mother woke up. I remember hearing my friend scream as the ER stapled her arm shut with no pain medicine because her family wasn't there yet, and they had to staple it shut.

I still, to this day, hear those screams thinking about it. I was ordered to go to a family court in Allen County. I attended court that day, and the judge wanted me to wait to get my license until I was 21, and he wanted me to clean out the back of ambulances that were covered in blood and puke. There wasn't anything available in Warren County like that for me to do. The judge issued me community service of 300+ hours at the adult day care cleaning up after the residence there. From that moment on, I knew I had to be someone my parents could be proud of, someone I was proud of, and someone my children one day would be proud of. When I saw how bad I hurt my parents for my pore choices, I knew I had to change my wild ways.

I did fail in my freshman year of high school because I didn't know I had ADHD. I just thought I was a failure at everything. Once I decided to get help, I was diagnosed with ADHD; I became focused. I was a freshman twice, became a sophomore, earned enough credits to skip my junior year, and was back on track with my class, and became a senior, and graduated early and with awards.

I met a wonderful man in my senior year of high school. He was inthe US Marine, and he was 4 years older than me. He was my best friend's cousin. He called her house one night to chat with her, and I happen to be at her house that night. He was lonely out in the desert and wanted someone to talk to. I gave him my phone number to call me some time. One night my mother made me stay home because my grandfather was visiting. This Marine I had started talking to briefly called me again that night. I answered the phone because, at the time, I felt I had nothing better to do. Thank goodness, I answered because he and I talked for 8 hours that night and fell in love. I had not met him yet in person. We had only spoken on the phone. I knew this was the man I was going to marry. After only 10 months of talking on the phone and not seeing each other very often because he was stationed in another state, we decided to get married. Only 3 days before I turned 18, on May 25, 2002, I married the man of my dreams.

Most people would think about how my husband and I met, and how young we were, we couldn't last. We have been happily married for over 12 years now. I think what has helped us to have such a successful marriage is because we did get married at a young age and we lived 12 + hours away from any family we had. We both matured as adults together. We hadn't yet figured out what my way was or his way was. We only had OUR way of life. We both have the same morals and values and respect. We communicate and love each other with our "Everything". If times were ever tough on us, we only had each other to depend on, and that made us stronger. We both have wonderful work ethics and great communication skills.

After about 5 years of a wonderful marriage and being just the 2 of us, we decided we were now ready to extend our family. We knew we would have trouble making a baby and that we would have to adopt. So, the best thing for us to make a family was for him to get out of the Marines and become a civilian. We decided to become foster/adoptive parents. I have had multiple surgeries on my bladder and ovaries, and my condition was making it difficult to conceive. We knew fostering was something we would be great at because we have big hearts and knew we could give children the home, love, family and structure they needed.

I am proud to say we adopted our son on March 10, 2009, and our daughter on April 20, 2010, and we are working on our 3rd adoption presently. The journey to adoption was very emotional, but all worth it. They say that the emotional roller coaster an adoptive parent goes through when adopting a child that is our "labor pains".

My journey is not over, there are more children out there in the world that need my love, and I plan on giving it to them. I plan on continuing in God's path he has given me and hopes that my life's experiences can help inspire other women to open up their hearts and homes. Dance like nobody is watching. Love like you have never been hurt! Sing like there is nobody listening. Work like you don't need the money. Live like it is *HEAVEN ON EARTH!*

JOURNEY 13

My journey has not been too tough as I have been blessed with a wonderful family. I am a product of divorced parents, but both who loved me and tried to give me what I needed but just couldn't make things work for themselves. I learned later in life not to be bitter about it because I would much rather them both be happy than to be miserable. However, I do think because of the divorce, I began to look for love in all of the wrong places at an early age and made a lot of mistakes early on. I married young when I didn't know exactly what I was looking for or what I wanted or needed in my life. However, as a result, I have 2 beautiful children, and I wouldn't trade them or this journey for anything in the world. But never would I have imagined I would be divorced with 2 children at the age of 43, but why not. It happens every day, and why am I so special or any different. I am an educated and successful Black woman. Could I be better? Yes. Could things be worse? Yes. But thank God, he has brought me to where I am today. I am happy. My children are healthy and happy, and I am blessed and highly favored. I struggled for many years with unhappiness and depression and really not knowing what to do with my life. As I mentioned, I married young, and although to my high school sweetheart, I really didn't know what love was. We grew up together, created these two beautiful children, one girl, and one boy but began to grow apart, and eventually wanted different things out of life. After 23 years, it was time for me to leave. It wasn't easy, and I felt as if I destroyed my children's lives, and I didn't know what to do or where to go. However, with God, family, and friends, and in that order, I have made it to the other side of happiness. The road hasn't been easy, and I am not quite sure what the future holds, but what I do know is that my steps are ordered by the Lord, and with him, I can't go wrong. I shall remain ever so faithful and wait until HE is finished with me. And with that being said, MY JOURNEY CONTINUES ON....

JOURNEY 14

My journey has been one fraught with difficulties, but I can say but God and smile. I was raised in a single-parent home by a young mother who decided that if she was woman enough to have me, she would be woman enough to take care and raise me the best she could. I have a wonderful support system in my mother, husband, daughter, mother-in-law, brother, and other family and friends. I have survived cervical cancer, had a tumor removed from my chest, and living with diverticulosis that has caused me to be admitted to the hospital on ten different occasions, with several of them being life-threatening. But God had not called my number yet. I have worked in a school district that I have worked my way from a paraprofessional to the Senior Director of Curriculum Implementation and Instructional Design for the entire school district in the past 20 years. I have learned that if I keep God first in all that I do, He would bless me and keep me. I can give all praise, glory, and honor to his Holy name for his goodness and mercy are shown towards me and my family. This life that we live is not a sprint; it is a marathon with may twist and turns. If we keep our eyes on the prize, which is Christ Jesus, he will see us to the finish line. I see the finish line as being in heaven, where I will be able to praise God from the rising of the sun to the going down of the same without life's interruptions.

JOURNEY 15

I got married in 1985, and was married for 26 years. Our son was born the first year, and my husband started drinking, running around, and partying. Soon, we started fighting, which led to physical and mental abuse. Though he never put his hands on our son, he left many bruises on me. My husband came from a church-going family; he had been raised his whole life in the church with Christian values. After about four years of the mess and living that sinful life, he decided to get back into the church, and we both accepted Jesus Christ as our Lord and Savior. I thought life was good. We bought a home, and then shortly after, our second child was born. We had a beautiful baby girl in 1989.

My husband was working, and I was working, so it felt like everything was coming together. My husband had a talent for musical instruments and played during church services; he'd also been called to preach. This meant that we traveled with the church to different places to worship God. Life was good, or so it seemed until his past caught up with our future. I found out that he had fathered two children, maybe three, during the time of our marriage. Since he was preaching at the time, he begged me to forgive him, which I acceded to. All the while, he paid child support and saw the children when he could behind my back. Our life went on, and I tried to piece my broken heart together. The other woman eventually married another man but didn't completely tell the truth to her husband about sleeping with a married man. Eventually, when the truth did come out, it really hurt her husband and their marriage. By this time, my husband had become the pastor of our church, and I was the First Lady of the church. I was still working on forgiveness, but God wasn't through with me yet. The other woman's husband went to jail, and then my husband started going back over to her house to see the kids, or so he claimed. As time went on, I felt something wasn't right, but I wanted to believe that a man who seemed so committed to God would be committed to me also.

The other woman, his "baby mama", and her children started coming to our church. It felt as if she was flaunting their relationship in my face. I knew something wasn't right. The day I found out they were still having an affair, I had been at church all day. I went to the other woman's trailer, knocked, and then entered. One of the kids said, daddy, your wife, is here". I walked back to the bedroom myself right behind his child that'd called for him. There he was in her room, lying on her bed with his shoes off. Apparently, this is what he called checking on the kids who were, by the way, aged 20, 23, and 24 years old. I said a few words that weren't exactly Godly and walked out. The next day, I filed for divorce. It's been five years since my divorce was final, and I want to say to all the preacher's wives and First Ladies of the church that you don't have to take it. If he's still messing up, just get out and move on with your lives. It doesn't matter what other people think or say. You have one life, and you deserve to be happy and treated right. Trust God, and it will be fine. Life currently for me is different now, and I LOVE it! I no longer have the hurt and stress about what he's doing because I'm now living life for me. I even went back to school, and I did open a small business for a short period of time until a major car factory called me. You see, my life isn't perfect, but I know who I am. So, at the end of the day, God's Grace and Mercy kept me. I mean my mind and soul and spirit.

You see, you don't have to be friends with the ones that hurt you, but you need to forgive, not for them, but for you. It is to FREE You!

JOURNEY 16

My journey through life has been full of love, family, and loads of experiences. Some were absolutely wonderful, and some were...not so wonderful but, I survived, and I'm still going strong by the grace of God.

There are so many things I could write about but, I want to share some of my experiences from a child to the woman I am today. I thought we were rich growing up because my parents did everything they could to give my brother and me a stable home environment. We went from living in the city on St. Ferdinand to the county on Reder. I thought we had hit the jackpot! We were "moving on up" just like Jefferson's! I had my own room, and I actually lived in it.

My mom had a heck of a time trying to get me to come out of that room. I would go to school, come home and go straight to my room. I had everything in there, but the kitchen sink. I had my beautiful white bedroom set trimmed in gold, with a corner desk for me to do my homework, my fluffy bed full of stuffed animals, my TV, and, of course, my dog, Ginger, who was my best friend. That dog went everywhere with me. She was my best friend and was always with me through every teenage heartache, sickness, and just life. I truly loved that dog as though she were my child.

As a child, I had to deal with issues of low self-esteem. I had long hair and a face full of freckles. I thought I was the ugliest thing that ever walked the face of the earth. I had so many freckles that I heard lemons would erase the freckles, so guess what? Yep, I rubbed lemons all over my face, and guess what else? It didn't work! I'm 51 years old, and I can honestly say that those suckers have multiplied ten times over! I started to wear glasses when I was around eight, and again, having heard that carrots would make your eyesight better; I ate carrots like there was no tomorrow, and once more, it didn't work. (I'm still blind as a bat to this day, but I love carrots!)

As a child, kids can be cruel and call you ugly, and those things stick to your mind like glue. When I decided to tell my mom how I felt, she thought I was absolutely crazy! "What in the world would make you say such a thing?" she asked. "You are not ugly; you are beautiful." She began to help me with embracing who I was and accepting my flaws. She would give me compliments and tell me I could do and be whatever I wanted. She encouraged and helped build my self- esteem.

A child with esteem issues will feel alone and unhappy, but the truth remains that everyone is beautiful in their own right. Beauty is not what or who you look like. Beauty is your heart and soul. Beauty is how you treat and encourage others to accept who they are. If you or someone you know is struggling with esteem issues, be a good friend, and steer them towards embracing their features, help them learn to be happy with themselves. Beauty is being able to accept every flaw, scar, and anything that you feel is not "perfect." We are not and never will be perfect,but, we can strive to be happy and accept what God has given us. God loves us and accepts us as we are; so, why can't we? All Women are unique in their own way, and it's up to us to dig deep and know that we are strong, we are invincible, and yes, we are women. Love and accept yourself, flaws, and all.

I can honestly say that I still struggle with a few issues,but, it is not the end of the world. I have grown into a healthy, happy, and absolutely wonderful person. I'm strong and full of confidence. Some may say I'm full of myself, but I prefer to think of it as being just a strong, confident woman who was taught to love herself no matter what.

JOURNEY 17

My journey started out on a very rough note. When I was 7, I lost my mother, who was 34 years old at the time. She left behind a husband and 6 little kids. My siblings and I were between the ages of 5 and 14. In fact, 5 (one child passed a couple of weeks after birth) of us were one year apart in age. The two eldest of us were 4 years apart. At an early age, I knew and understood things beyond measure. For example, at the age of 7, I knew in my heart, my mother was going to die. I remember standing at the foot of her bed, watching her suffer from a phenomenon (unknown to my mother). My mother was the kind of woman who took care of her kids while self-medicating on over the counter medications. Ironically, the day she passed away, she was scheduled to see the doctor that same morning. She passed away August 1974 in our Nashville, TN home.

After my mother passed, my father moved us to Chicago, Illinois. Before we were to move with my father, he purchased a big home for all of us to live in. While my father was preparing our home, three of the children lived with my father's mother, and the other three lived with my mother's mother. This living arrangement was for about a year and a half. After I started high school, my life journey took me down the path of a naive and scared teenage mother at the age of 17. I dropped out of high school after I moved back to Nashville to live with my sister Annette Owens. It was my intention to get my GED as soon as I arrived in TN. However, things did not go as planned for the first year. Needless to say, I did get my GED in 1989. During this time in my life, I learned what it meant to struggle financially and emotionally.

For example, while I had some family members that were very supportive, I also had many family members to remind me of my mistakes at an early age. I know what it feels like to feel alone while pregnant and judged. These judgments came from family, peers, and church members. Throughout my journey, I have dealt with some losses that shook me to my very core. I lost my 21-year old brother in 1990, and two sisters (the oldest siblings) within 9 months of each other. One passed in 2004 and the other in 2005. These journeys have taught me how to be a strong person while dancing to the beat of my OWN drum. I don't sweat the small things because I know tomorrow is not promised.

I always look on the bright side of everything. The most important thing throughout my journey is my strong faith in God. Without him, I would be NOTHING. I continue to self-reflect while understanding my life journey. This includes the good, bad, and the ugly. I truly believe there are lessons in everything we do. It is up to us to take heed and act accordingly. I also learned that forgiveness goes a long way. Forgiveness not only produces growth, but it also increases one's strength. Thus, I have forgiven myself as well as others a long time ago.

Along this journey, I have accomplished a lot. For instance, I am married to the love of my life for 16 years and counting. I also have five beautiful grandchildren and 6 awesome kids. I currently have 6 more months before I graduate with my Bachelors in Business Administration with a concentration in Human Resources. I obtained my Real Estate license in 2002; additionally, I worked for a wonderful company as a sales representative for 14 Years. This journey enables me to learn an unmeasurable amount of knowledge and skills. Today I continue to look for ways to better myself and others positively. I have learned many things about myself throughout my journey, and I welcome the opportunity to learn and grow further.

While this is only a small part of my journey, I pray that will uplift and help others who may be going through some things in their life. In the end, we choose our own destiny, and I refuse to let others write my story.

JOURNEY 18

My journey is still in the full course. As a divorcee, I am in the process of reinventing myself. I've learned a lot and lost a lot, but I'm not throwing in the towel yet! One of my favorite poets wrote, "what happens to a dream deferred?" The poem gives many scenarios of what happens to a dream deferred, and I like to believe that one day, I will actualize my dreams. As I access my present situation, I must admit that I often wonder how I got here. I spent nearly 20 years in a relationship that brought me years of personal sacrifice and dysfunction while working towards something that my partner had long given up on but forgot to tell me. I will give credit that out of this relationship, I was blessed with three beautiful children, but man, do I have so many battle scars! The war is not yet over, and as I plan to 'Get Up', I must admit that the battle was lost. I loved it; it was hard, and, for a long time, the center of my existence. But I now see the error of my ways. I spent so much time and energy trying to make the most of a bad situation. While my spirit was broken, I have lost over 100lbs, and I'm ready to live again. I want to see the splendor of my dreams. I am presently working on regaining my footing, praying, and seeking God for my next move! My dream is to become a Nurse Midwife and eventually teach nursing. I'm currently going to nursing school while working and taking care of my twin teenage girls.

Some days I feel this dream is insurmountable, then I remind myself that nothing beats a failure, but a try! My dreams definitely deferred, but not denied! I am battling my way back! At this time, I have three thriving college students, one at U of L, IIT Chicago, and MTSU. Recently I had my name changed and gave up my ex-name, and I'm taking my life back! I realized there's a joy to be had in whatever situation or circumstance I find myself in. I've moved from Victim to Victor, my mess is now a message, and my tragedy is now a triumph! What's impossible with man is possible with God, and I shall succeed because I AM ENOUGH!

JOURNEY 19

I was born to Donald & Thelma Ford. My parents divorced early, they had four children, and the first child died, leaving three children: myself, Timothy, and Pam. My childhood was a very hard one at times because I was the oldest and therefore seemed to be aware of the things that were going on. However, if I could go back and change the hands of time, I wouldn't change a thing.

My journey as a teenager with a mother who was mentally ill was very difficult. During my early teen years, I begin to notice things my mother was saying and doing that didn't seem to be normal. I never talked about it to anyone, but I often wondered if other people noticed it. This went on for a while through my high school years. It seemed that after high school, things started to get worse with my mother. I remember one day I received a call that my uncle had my mother committed. This was very hard on me, and I didn't want to accept it even though I knew it was good for her in order to ensure her getting better. I went on with life as though nothing had happened, and when my mother was released, things seemed to be back to normal and better for a while. Then one day, I started noticing things she was doing and saying again. This time I was a lot older, so I knew it was up to me to figure out the best options for my mother. One day, I knew it was time, and I would need to have her committed again. I also knew that I would have to rely on Jesus. I felt so bad inside, but outside I behaved as if life was usual because I needed to be strong for my siblings with my baby and husband. The entire situation always had me on my knees, praying, asking God to help me and for it not to happen to me. I would pray for his hand to cover my mother and my life and God just what I asked of him.

Even during my Mother's mental illness, she would always tell me to forgive, pray and call on Jesus. I learned that from my mother, and it has become part of my life. No matter how difficult it is, I will forgive others and ask God always to forgive me.

You must constantly pray and call on Jesus and remember to forgive.

Proverbs 3:5-6 Trust in the Lord with all thine heart and lean not unto thine own understanding. In all thy ways acknowledge him, and he shall direct thy paths.

JOURNEY 20

I have always prayed to God for a job to be able to take care of my daughter as a single mother. God blessed me dearly in 1999 with a very good job. My next was to meet a God-fearing man. I met someone that appeared to be concerned about my health and gave me the knowledge to buy a house, so I bought my first home. This person didn't love God the way I did, so I tried to get away from him. God sent a spirit-filled man in my life once more. In February 2007, my mother passed away, and I was going through a difficult time in my life. The man in my life seemed to help me through this time, and he seemed okay, but not exactly what I asked God for. Soon, he gave me an engagement ring. To me, something still wasn't right. I felt it in my gut that something wasn't right. (Make sure that you always go by your first reaction, especially if you feel something is just not right). As it turned out, I was right about this man; he wasn't being honest with me, but I didn't find out until after his death. Yes, he died in 2007, and it was another difficult time for me to get through the unexpected death along with the other things he had been hiding from me. I was able to shake it off and get through this situation. So now, what God? Well, the next year in February 2008, I met a God-fearing man who asked me about my past relationship and my fiancé. I told him that he passed away recently. He couldn't believe what he was hearing. I think his first reaction or comment was, "WHAT?" He told me to call him if I needed someone to talk to. We became friends, and we talked, and he helped me throughout this process. In May 2008, he took me to The Smokey Mountains and told me that he "He loved me". In December 2008, I married the man of my dreams. The man I asked God to bring to me.

Praise God!

Just be careful what and who you pray for. Life doesn't always go according to our plans, but in God's ordinance and most definitely his time. Always stay in the word no matter what, and stay true to his word. There are a time and season for everything in life, so remain faithful. He never forgets the promises he makes to you. "Seasons" by Donald Lawrence was my wedding song. May God bless and keep you as you read this. Make sure that you Love you and also love Jesus.

JOURNEY 21

I married the guy that I had the heaviest crush on in high school, 14 years later, after 2 kids, it didn't work. I wanted it to work so bad that when it didn't, I held on to so much guilt and anger. It took me a long time to forgive the situation, forgive myself, and finally forgive him so that I could be free to use that energy to make room for something big. In the year 2000, I moved my 2 young children to Alabama and raised them alone. We discovered my mother was in stage 4 of non-Hodgkin's lymphoma, and I signed my divorce papers. I did not want to leave my parents at that time, but the company I worked for relocated from Mississippi to Alabama. This was a tough period; I felt like I was having an out of body experience. I traveled most weekends to see my mother while in and out of the hospital. I could not believe that this was happening to my mother. In 2003 Mother's Day weekend, the angels took her away. Shortly after, my father also passed on with a series of small illnesses, but I'm sure it was a broken heart. As it goes, they were soul mates who grew up together. I miss them so much. I discussed so much with them and looked to them for advice on marriage and raising a family. I went through a period of about 5-7 years of straight stress. After my mother passed, I began to have panic attacks and had to get on two prescriptions to manage my blood pressure. She was my rock, my counselor, and held all the answers; even when I made poor decisions, she still supported me with wisdom and unconditional love. In some of her hardest final days, I remember her saying, "I don't know why I keep holding on." I finally gathered up enough nerves to say, "it's ok, it's ok...we will be ok." My heart was so heavy that evening; I drove back to Birmingham, crying all 360-miles back home. Knowing that she would not be the same the next time I saw her.

Someone once said that God picks the prettiest flowers to help the other ones grow. Between 2003-2005 I had night terrors; I would jump out of bed running at least once a week. The next day I would find bruises on my legs or waist from hitting the edge of my bed. After about 18 months, one night, I prayed and asked God to deliver me from night terrors, and he did. One night I was watching late-night TV and ran across one of my favorite movies, "Shawshank Redemption". One scene from that movie that I loved was when Andy would not allow grim circumstances (prison) to keep him from hoping and following his dreams. He felt like he had two options in life: get busy living or get busy dying.

At that moment, I woke up! I thought, Linda, *Get Busy Living*. I started making small changes, doing things for myself, putting myself at least 2nd instead of last (Kids 1st), working out, losing weight, meeting people, girls night out, heck even a girl's vacation, and even managed to throw in new male friends. My journey is the DNA of my character. My experiences helped me manage my insecurities. It took a while, but I've learned much about me. I understand that true happiness comes when loving myself while constantly changing to become a better me. I understand that my main purpose is to pour as much love, knowledge, and 'mommisums' into my kids as I can while here on earth. That's the job God assigned me to as a parent. And above all, I'm thankful for God's grace and mercy.

And I pray that he continues to see me through.

With Love, to all my sisters from the same mother, and sisters from another mother.

Behind The Mirror

JOURNEY 22

Every little girl has a dream of getting married to a prince one day. After being in a toxic relationship for many years, I decided to step out on faith and take my children and run. I never looked back. The fear of raising two small children on my own was terrifying, and my dream of getting married to someone that loved me for me was pretty much over, so I thought. I put my life on the back burner to focus on my kids. It was not an easy road, but I made it. I could finally see the light at the end of the tunnel. I was able to get the oldest graduated and out of the house, and then my youngest had two years left in school. They didn't seem to need me as much anymore, so I decided to take a little time for myself. I was able to get back into the world after being gone for so many years. Man, was it a struggle. I had trust issues, and I had built a wall. I made a promise to myself that I would not let anyone in again. I was not going to be hurt by a man ever again. After a few dates, I decided to give up. I prayed about it and turned it over to God. When I least expected, I met this great man. I had seen him before, but couldn't figure out where I knew him from. We started talking, and when it came to me that I knew his brother. His brother lived across the walkway from me. We've been together ever since the first date. He accepts me for me, and he loves me unconditionally in spite of my flaws. He loves my kids as much as he loves his own kids. We pray together; we pray for each other and our families. He motivates and inspires me to step out of my comfort zone to do bigger things in life. We have been together for 7 years, and we have been married for 3 of those 7 years. I must say I'm having the time of my life being married to him. It's not always peaches and cream, but I couldn't see myself on this journey with anyone else. With that being said, I'm glad I waited on God to send me this man to be a part of my life.

JOURNEY 23

My favorite saying and bible verse is: Luke 17:21, when Jesus said *"the kingdom of God is within you."* If I didn't know that the kingdom was within me – that grace beyond the material world – creating, guiding and demonstrating as infinite potential, I would not have the conviction to accomplish what I am called to do. We are not separate from but are "one" with this divine source of absolute good. I grew up in the grace of witnessing the flow of infinite power blessing me at each turning point, teaching me that we are here to realize God's full potential by being our best for everyone and everything in the universe. With grace, even what appear to be burdens become our greatest gifts. Even what appear to be challenges make our journeys worthwhile.

I grew up in the Jefferies Housing Project in Detroit. When I pass by the space where it stands, it is hard for me to imagine it containing so many lives born there, nurtured there, educated there, matured there, and – if fortunate – empowered there. Many could not see beyond what now appear to have been no more than 7 or 8 blocks of bricks. I never counted them as they seemed to go on endlessly, until I looked up lying in the grass in our front lawn one day – stretched out under the Sycamore tree with its white bark peeling, and I saw that the horizon was infinite –. When I was young and very flexible, I could bend forward and look up – beyond Mrs. Hopson's apple tree and see magnificent clouds above the fray. As the Psalmist says *"I will lift up my eyes to the mountains; from where shall my help come? My help comes from the Lord"*. My help comes from an unlimited wellspring of love that pulls us beyond the unpredictable to the amazing.

Childhood for me was short-lived in some respects and in others–has never ended. I grew up in the sixties to a Captain Kangaroo morning of Cheerios that ended abruptly when President John F. Kennedy, Jr. was assassinated. I have never forgotten the day. It was cool and gray, and Rocky and Bullwinkle went off forever, followed by the assassination of Malcolm X, Robert Kennedy, Martin Luther King, the Detroit public school teachers on strike, and the Detroit riots. All of that was wrapped in the harsh reality of realizing that my father was mentally ill and would not get better. The bus rides to Ypsilanti State Hospital were only upstaged by the U.S. Army jeeps that patrolled the freeways and streets of Detroit when the looting started in 1967. By the time I was 10, I had learned to fall to the floor quickly when I heard the sounds of guns and had witnessed everything from heroin needles to prostitutes selling their wares on skid row. I remember my mother teaching me to read by three but continuing to read to us Harriet Tubman, Sojourner Truth and about the killings at Kent State University. I wanted to be a Hippie when I grew up–making love, not war and perhaps dress like a Black Panther with a huge afro, dancing to Marvin Gaye and the Stylistics until my daddy came home from the hospital, and left my mother with five kids and no money: four brothers, and me. By then, I was 11 years old, working for the Model Cities Program, making $20 a week, which I used to pay my way to Girl Scout camp and buy my school clothes. I've been working ever since.

By 12, I made a decision. I could try to run with the popular kids–who always seemed to wear nice clothes and have spending money, or I could take the less traveled path of a commitment to excellence in school despite the harsh reality that I would have to take this journey alone. I had already skipped from kindergarten to second grade and probably should have skipped a few more because none of my peers knew what I was talking about. I was blessed with brothers who attended a summer program at Cranbrook, a private prep boarding

Behind The Mirror

school in Bloomfield Hills, Michigan through Horizons Upward Bound. Back then there were no programs for girls in Detroit. So, I awaited their return and the return of their friends and read everything that they did. By the grace of God, I decided to take the less-traveled path.

In some respects, my childhood reminds me of the season of the hit TV series 'The Wire' that was never written. Yes, there is a season in that poignant story of drugs and crime and death in Baltimore that should have been written and never was. Somehow the writers, perhaps because they never lived the story that they told, never told the truth about the women who live in the drug-infested inner cities—women who not only survive but insure the survival of their children despite the odds. Like many other children in the 'hood, I was blessed to have a great mother in not only my "Mama," but in Mrs. Wilson, Mrs. Ford, Mrs. Hamilton, Mrs. Benson, Mrs. Greene, Mrs. Troutman, Mrs. Johnson, Mrs. Malone, Mrs. Hunt, Mrs. Boynton, Mrs. McGraw, Aunt Essie, and so many other mothers who lived only a few feet away and shared their generosity as well as their guidance. When my mother worked, and went to school and could not attend the award day or the conference, her friends stepped in. Someone would always be there.

The best thing about being 13 was meeting my niece for the first time. Like many other Detroiters, we headed to the south during the summer to visit relatives. We have relatives in South Carolina and Kentucky, as well as several other states, but we only visited Kentucky where we stayed with our Aunt Fannie. I loved Aunt Fannie because she had a whistling voice that was always filled with excitement and sunshine. You could wear her words and dance in their deliverance as she drove her Cadillac up and down red dirt roads dropping in on funeral parlors to see what Miss 'So and So' was wearing as she lay there in the casket–and then, we were off! I never thought of the fact that it was my own aunt who took me to see my niece Ti'Sha, who was then three. I didn't really know my sister as she was almost a generation older and was the daughter of my father's first wife. But Aunt Fannie was wise enough to know that we needed to make that connection with our niece, and so she took us to her great aunt's house, where she lived. I just remember her standing there, pretty and brown and part of us–and I am sure if we were old enough, we would have come back to visit her and carry her and be a good aunt and uncles. But we were too young, and so instead I carried her in my heart, in my prayers, and in God's grace. There probably has not been a single moment that I did not think of her, and bless her, and love her.

The next thing I knew, I was at Cass Technical High School, at 13. It was one of the most difficult transitions of my life but also one of the most profound. It was where I saw myself for the first time in the larger world. It was one of the first times I knew that I lived in a place where others were afraid to go. At first, I withdrew into a quiet orbit of insecurity, trembling when I spoke–and allowing myself to believe that because someone's parents could buy them the most fashionable shoes and even a car, they had something more profound to say. Fortunately, I flew from that cocoon with new wings of strength and purpose. Ralph Waldo Emerson, Charles Roth and Kenneth Jones were my best friends. I read Emerson's 'Essays' and Roth's 'Mind: The Master Power', but Kenneth was my friend who sat behind me and pulled my two long braids until I turned around and punched him, and we became friends for life. He was a journalist even then, who eventually went to the University of Michigan in Ann Arbor and to New York City to attend Columbia University's Masters program in Journalism, writing for the New York Times and for so many publications until he passed away in 2007. As kids in Detroit, Kenneth and I were always out and about–interviewing everyone from Lily Tomlin, who his mother knew, to Chaka Kahn. We even barged in on poet and publisher Dudley Randall one night, at his home, and he gave us orange juice to drink while we talked about his publishing company Broadside Press.

Mrs. Francis Hamburger was my first mentor. She was my public speaking coach. She taught me to trust my own voice and be a witness to my own story. She gave me the first opportunity to record for the first time in a professional studio. She sent a white judge one time to the projects to pick me up, and it was the first time I rode in such a nice car where someone played classical music. I had very large afro puffs at the time, which my mother thought was probably one reason I did not win that day, even though I was the best. I was the only black participant. But one day, Mrs. Hamburger asked me which college I wanted to attend – out of my top choices. "Howard University is my number one choice," I said. Shortly thereafter, I was awarded a full scholarship to Howard University, all expenses paid. Mrs. Hamburger was a white woman, but she will always be one of my ancestors: a mother, friend, and mentor to many if not all of her students.

The truth about black people in this country is that we were enslaved by a society that refuses to acknowledge that we are all from the same village, just as white as we are black, just as brown as we are yellow, just as tan as we are red: race is a construct. The myth that we are racialized bodies from different tribes was created to justify inhumanity, greed, and exploitation. We are all from the same mother. I recently had my DNA tested. I not only have ancestors from Nigeria and Ghana and Togo and Benin and the Cameroons and South Africa, but also from Great Britain and Finland and East Asia and the Middle East, and ancestors who are indigenous natives to this country.

At Howard University, I continued to study the contributions of people everywhere. After Howard, where I received a BFA (1980) and created the first major in Theater Management, I got an MFA from UCLA in Theater Management (1982), then a Juris Doctor from New York University School of Law (1985), where I served as Managing Editor for the Review of Law & Social Change. Many years later, I received my Master of Divinity from New York Theological Seminary (2007). I am 61 years young, and I feel as though I grow younger each day. I am co-creator and pastor of a church in New York City called *SPIRITMUV® Church-in-Motion*, www.spiritmuv.com, a trans-denominational church-in-motion, which means that everyone is welcome to our virtual app and can "have church" wherever they are.

I am co-creator of *God is a Brown Girl Too®*, a ministry for the self-empowerment of women (https://godisabrowngirltoo.wordpress.com/). My book, *'God is a Brown Girl Too',* in which God speaks to black women as themselves, says, "when you know that that I am you, and you are me–you will begin to realize who God is." God's grace is the victory of the divine potential within each and every one of us–regardless of race or gender or age or ability or sexual preference or religion or nationality or politics or wealth or employment status or any other factor pertaining to the material world.

I realized that I was on a journey of grace when I was in the hospital at 17 and the doctors didn't think I would make it, but I did. I was in pain every day for several months but would imagine myself in the arms of Jesus Christ. I knew then that I would live to write. I just had no idea how extraordinary the grace of God could write as me, and I am still amazed. The first book that I wrote is called, *The Soul Sings to Her Mother,* a short book that I wrote in an hour or two for children of all ages; it is now a featured poem in my first book of poetry entitled *Unbroken Circles*. The first book that I published, however, was my mother's book, *Angels, Angels Everywhere*. It was a surprise because she had long wanted to publish. I formed a publishing company named, in part, after her–called <u>Myrtle Tree Press LLC</u>, in order to publish the first children's book that she wrote. Her second book, in the same genre, is called, *The Angel Blanket*. Both are available on Amazon and Barnes and Noble and are beautifully illustrated children's books.

My own books include *Prayers for Those Standing on the Edge of Greatness; God is a Brown Girl Too; Ten Laws of Unlimited Success,* and my first novel, *God is a Lawyer Too,* as well as *Seeing Myself as God Sees Me* and others. I try to publish at least one book per year. My retreats include published workbooks. Even when I am not publishing, I am writing a book. I am working on three this year. People always ask me how to get publish, and I say that the first thing you need to do is write for me, that means writing as if my life requires it.

I know that I am here to do God's work, which requires me to get up at 5 A.M. every morning and listen in the silence for God's word. God's word is not necessarily a voice or a message, it is an experience. I meditate daily and have a free online meditation because it is one of the most sacred practices. As the Psalmist said, "be still and know that I am God." The daily meditation can be accessed at the following website: *https://mindfulnessgroup.blog/*. Miracles have taken place in the lives of those who use it. All you have to do is sign up, and I send you a free link to the meditation website. These are guided meditations; but we also meditate by being still and knowing that we are one with the divine. After we meditate, we are in synch with the grace of inexhaustible supply, universal intelligence and unconditional love. We step into the kingdom of supernatural healing, power, and prosperity–the realization that we always have everything we need.

Some people ask me how did I end up in theater, but the truth is that it is a remarkable foundation for ministry and the law. Not only are you required to perform in both professions, but you are also required to be well-organized and disciplined. Theater is never about the final production, it is about the dedication and work that contributes to it. The saying "the show must go on" is true. I know what it takes to stay the course because I have been blessed with the background of writing, directing, stage-managing, producing, and performing for the theatre. God has prepared me for being on call, responding on my feet, creating on the fly, and speaking from wherever I stand—not only through law or management or writing—but from taking a show from beginning to end. Now, that's grace.

Grace blesses my journey with balance. When I teach the scripture about Jacob (Mind) and Esau (Body) and the former steals his brother's birthright, I explain that there must be balance between the two. The scripture shows us that ultimately Jacob had to pay for what he did to his brother. We must take care of our body temples. We are temples of the living God. This means that I try to work out six days a week. But I only do what I really enjoy doing. I lift weights at the gym three days a week—for one to two hours, training each body part. I also do cardio at least once a day. My current goal is to get at least 10,000 steps in each day by walking. My challenge is maintaining good, clean eating habits. I try to eat produce, the food that is organic and alive, rather than manmade. I also try to get at least six hours of sleep, naps if I can and try to drink at least eight glasses of water each day. I try to limit the meals where I do eat to salads and fish or chicken, boiled eggs and apples. Eating healthy, drinking plenty of water, getting enough sleep, and exercise is the best beauty treatment that there is, accompanied by proper nutrition for the soul.

We cannot experience grace unless we are spiritually fit. The only way to attain spiritual fitness is through daily meditation. Jesus says seek first the kingdom of God and all else will follow. In the various wildernesses that I have experienced, I wanted my daily manna but I thought it was material bread–money in my pocket, food on the table, clothes to wear, a job to do. But then I realized that manna is through the kingdom that is always blessing us. When we are tapped in and turned on to the power in us, we are tapped in and turned on to the bread of life, which is the manna of endless source and infinite supply.

When we grow in the consciousness of Christ, our love life follows too. Our soul mates stand before our very eyes if we are discerning enough to see them. We have to be honest when we marry. One of the most challenging times of my life was being with a man who did not share my values. He was materially successful but did not know God. He once told me that I was "procrastinating" by meditating. After a lot of prayer and meditation and affirmations, I had the courage to move forward in grace. I talk about the importance of loving grace in release and forgiveness as we journey through in life in my book _Prayers for Those Standing on the Edge of Greatness_. Fourteen years after I left, he passed away. Long before he passed, I met and married Marlon Cromwell, who is one of the most loving, supportive people I know.

Here is another example of grace. Before my ex-husband passed away, I published _God is a Lawyer Too_. Grace led me to an image to use for my cover. Only after the book was in print did I look at the man on the cover walking away into the horizon and realize that the photo looked exactly like my ex-husband. When he passed away, I thought about the synchronicity of him in the photograph as though moving forward on the book cover–in his typical lawyerly suit, carrying his typical briefcase. It was distributed around the time that he made his transition. Months later, he spoke to me in a dream and said that he did not have long but wanted to tell me one thing. He said "we are accountable for all things," and he went up into the sky. Here was a man who never appeared to know God, bringing me a biblical verse. I found Romans 3:19, which says, *"now we know that whatever the law says, it says to those who are under the law, so that every mouth may be silenced and the whole world held accountable to God."* I realize now that the scripture was the soul of the book: that we are on our journeys for a reason and are held accountable for accomplishing it.

Being accountable to God requires us to be in the presence of God, requires us to be diligent about seeking the Kingdom of God, requires us to realize that grace is not of this world and thus has no limitation. I am accountable to God through my ministry (https://spiritmuvblog. com/), which teaches the word of Spirit and Truth. I am accountable to my extended family of all those whom I meet. I am accountable to living a life of spiritual fitness–in body, mind, and soul. I am accountable to Jesus Christ for calling me to minister through the Word.

When I was 41 years old, Jesus came to me in a vision and told me, "I carried you on your sick bed, I carried you when you didn't have a job, I carried you when you went through your divorce, I carried you through every trial and tribulation: *What makes you think I would leave you now?"*

Perhaps in some way, I realized from the very moment as a child, when I stared up into the heavens of blue sky and white clouds, that I would be summoned to teach that God is everywhere present and that everyone is on a journey of grace.

As *God is Brown Girl Too* says "Move forward on this journey–like never before. Enjoy the blessing of realizing that you control your life, that everything is coming together for your greatest good, that there is nothing that you cannot do, that Spirit is pulling you outside the box of limitation and lifting you in a new dimension of change, that the sun is radiating from your soul, and that your sisters are here leading the way." This is my prayer, that you too come to know God's grace and allow it to embrace you, and anoint you and bless you, and favor you—like never before.

JOURNEY 24

Throughout my life, I've been blessed considerably. As a child, I was raised in a small town by two of the best Christian parents. They taught me to always put God and my church first in life; do unto others as you'd have them do unto you; work hard; be honest; pay my debts; respect is earned; to follow my gut instinct—it won't lead me wrong, and if something isn't worth doing right it isn't worth doing at all. These mottos directed me through my adolescence, teenage and college years. Since children aren't brought into this world with a manual, I've relied on those inspirational words of wisdom to guide me in raising my three, handsome sons.

Fourteen-years-ago, my gut instinct led me through the most terrifying and humbling experience of my life. Our second son was born on March 29, 2005. We were overjoyed! He was so beautiful and seemed perfect, but he wasn't a content baby. I tried everything that I could think of to pacify him. Nothing seemed to work. He fussed day and night. When he was six-weeks-old, he developed a cough that sounded more like a bark, and he would cry until he'd be dripping with sweat. My gut told me something was wrong. We took him to the doctor three times a week, begging for answers. Finally, on the third visit—they admitted him to a local hospital for overnight observation.

Upon admission, the CNA attempted to take his blood pressure. She kept insisting that the reading wasn't accurate, or the cuff was too big because there was no pressure in his legs and extreme pressure in his arms. They took him for a chest x-ray, EKG and ECG and found nothing. They set up an oxygen tent, and for the first time in his life, he slept six straight hours. They released him and sent him home the following day, which was coincidental— Friday, May 13th. They told us that he had colic, a small PDA, and instructed me not to research what it meant. That was like telling me to research it as quickly as possible, and I found that he had a cardiac problem, and of course, the panic set in.

After spending one night at home, we were back to square one. My son wasn't getting any better, and I was at my wit's end. I slept in the recliner, holding him upright, and I told my husband that he was going to die if someone didn't help us. My in-laws had a neighbor at their lake house who was a Pediatric-Cardio Surgeon at Kosair Children's Hospital. They gave me his number, and I called him on Saturday and explained my son's symptoms. He told me that fortunately, a group of pediatric cardiologists came to Bowling Green once a month, and they were coming on the following Wednesday. He told me to take him there at 9 am along with a copy of the test that was performed at the local hospital.

Just as the doctor advised, we took him to the appointment, and in just five minutes, I heard words that I wasn't prepared for. During the ECG reading, the physician told me that my 7-week-old baby boy had a *bicuspid aorta valve and coarctation of the aorta* and needed to have open-heart surgery immediately. I went numb. They told us to drive him to Kosair's Emergency Room, and they'd be waiting for us there.

We arrived at the ER, and they put the chest x-ray from the local hospital on the lights. The MD said, "This baby also has congestive heart failure. He should be dead." My baby was drinking his bottle as they took his blood pressure and it was 177/123 in his right arm. They immediately got him started him on intravenous Lasix, and his diapers weighed unbelievably.

Two days later, on May 20th, he had open-heart surgery. He was in ICU for 5 days and on the floor for 5 days. During that time, I called on everyone that I knew to please pray for our baby. I remember well bowing on the floor of the bathroom in the hospital and telling the Lord if He'd take care of our baby, I'd serve Him the rest of my life. I felt selfish for that prayer and soon told him that whether he healed my baby or not, I'd still serve Him. I felt so helpless, and all I knew to do was depend on God and the prayers of my family and friends for strength. Through God's mercies, my son came home on May 27.

While we were at Kosairs, three children died around my son in ICU. Sick children with ongoing diseases and conditions surrounded us. Just thought of 'what could have been' or what we saw other families enduring while we were at Kosairs quickly changes life's perspective.

My son just turned 14. He's healthy, thriving, an honor student, athletic, and recently saved during our last revival. What more could I ask for? He has annual follow-up appointments with Pediatric Cardiology, but otherwise has no restrictions.

This was the most humbling journey of my life, but one that I pray that I never have to experience again.

JOURNEY 25

My life has been pretty easy and simple. I didn't grow up facing any challenges. I come from a single-parent household, but I had the best family I could ask for. I didn't long for anything, and I pretty much got everything I wanted. I graduated high school, went on to attend/ graduate college. I had a job offer a week after graduating. I relocated to a new city. I have been able to travel and see the world. I have been surrounded by good people who have had my back and been supportive. I can honestly say I have good friends. One of the most exciting times of my life was overshadowed by stress, unemployment, disappointment, and foolishness. For the first time in my life, I didn't know how I was going to make it nor what I was going to do, but God saw me through. I am not a "holy roller or Bible Beater!" All the terms associated with religious people. I am a spiritual person, and I know what God has done for me. I know how he answers my prayers, and I know how he gives me peace that truly surpasses my own understanding. Just when I thought things could get worse, doors began to open, and life got back on track. People try various things to seek comfort. Drugs, alcohol, promiscuity etc. None of that will fill the void that you seek.

My Journey is that God brought me through when no one else could. Just that simple!

JOURNEY 26

Let me start by saying that you are not alone. God put all of us here for a reason and purpose in mind. It's not easy to understand at times, but if you listen and pay attention, you will figure it out. I struggle to this day trying to figure things out instead of letting it happen. The reason that I'm able to create this book of journeys is that it's to help other women. For several years, I knew that I should be able to help people in some form, but I just couldn't figure out how this was going to be accomplished. *FEAR* sometimes makes us doubt our ability to accomplish our goals. Fear can be so intimidating that it stops your blessing when it's right in front of you. I want to take you on a little journey and show you those things that seem impossible never should stop you from thinking that it's possible.

As a little girl, I always loved being around my mother and watching her interact with people. I was always so shy around other people, and she seemed to have no problem talking with anyone. My mother was very nurturing and calm even when she was upset about something. I remember a few incidents at school that caused my mother to be called to come to school. As I said before, I was a very shy child, and, most of the time, would go with the flow when interacting and playing with other kids. One day, at recess in 3rd grade, we went out to play, and we started playing a game that I don't quite remember, but I was winning. I was very happy, but one of my classmates wasn't happy, and he called me a name. Most of the time, if you were called a name, it wasn't really that big of a deal. That's just part of kids growing up - calling each other names. This time it was a big deal to me! It seemed as if the world had stopped turning for those few seconds, and my only focus was the face of my classmate. This person I played with every day at recess and felt was my friend had stepped across the line today. Not only did he call me a name that was degrading, but he had broken our friendship. The name he called me simply because I was winning the game. The 'N' word (which is even hard for me to type the word right now). Within those few seconds, I remember thinking did I blackout because I didn't feel anything moving in my body, but my eyes were still focused on my classmate. Ok, so I must still be awake? All I could hear were kids in the background who seemed so far away telling other kids to "go get a teacher! Go get the teacher!" I stood there without moving from that exact same spot, and my eyes latched onto my classmate. It seemed like hours before a teacher arrived, but as I stood there with my fist balled up, I wasn't going to move one step. Within those few seconds, I had hit my classmate and busted his nose. This incident seemed like it took forever, but looking back, I know it was only a few seconds that this all occurred. I remember standing there with my fist so tight that I had fingernail marks on my right palm. I watched as he cried and tears streaming down his face while he held his nose. Other kids ran to get the teacher, while some stood looking on at me as I saw him holding his nose with the blood streaming down his face mixed with blood and tears going onto his uniform in what appeared to me to be slow motion. The blood in my veins continued to pump stronger and louder throughout my body. I could hear my heart pumping so loud I thought others might hear it as well. I knew that I would probably be in trouble, but I also knew that I will always stand up for myself and what's right for the rest of my life.

At that moment, I understood that I will always stand up for what's right shy or not. My next issue was dealing with the nuns at our school (I went to a Catholic School). I loved attending the Catholic School, but the nuns just didn't quite understand why I took the path of violence over talking through the problem. Especially from a girl that never caused any problems and was sometimes too shy to answer questions in class. As the nuns rushed to assist my classmate with his nose, I was quickly taken to the office. As I thought about the trouble, I might be in; I still felt calm and confident. This reaction was strange to me because I've never been taught to hit anyone unless I was defending myself. As I waited for my mother to arrive, in that I knew that she wouldn't be happy because she had to leave work.

I had plenty of time to think about how I handled the situation. I pondered if I made the right decision, and I knew I probably made the wrong one. The nuns continued to talk to each other in the other room while they kept looking back at me with a strange look on their face. For a moment, I thought they might make me go to mass to repent my sins. I would probably need to do 50 'Our Fathers' and 50 'Hail Marys' after I repented. I was just playing through all the scenarios in my mind. My mother arrived and apparently didn't know exactly what happened except that I hit another kid.

When she came, the look she gave me was not a look of anger or disappointment, which caught me off guard. I was still looking down, holding onto the side of the wooden chair that I was told to sit in. I felt ashamed, but I felt this way not because I hit my classmate, but because my mother had to take a taxi all the way to my school and leave her class for someone else to teach while she was away. She worked very hard, and I felt bad that I messed up her day. As she sat down beside me, she looked at me again and smiled. My mother then took her hand and placed it under my chin and said, raise your head up and don't look down. I sat up in my chair and raised my head up with more confidence. She proceeded to ask the nuns what happened that caused her daughter to hit another student? The nuns started to tell my mother about the other little boy and about his nose. My mother said, "that's not what I asked you. I asked what happened that would make my child hit another student?" The nuns looked surprised at my mother's response. I remember them responding that this was a serious issue that I hit another child. At that point, she said, "I completely understand that it's a serious situation; that's the reason I'm sitting in this seat". "Tell me why my daughter hit another child?" "What events took place to lead to this situation?" The nuns seemed stunned that she would ask such questions. My mother looked at me and then asked me, "what happened, and why did you hit another student?" I told her everything that happened to the point where he called me a name. She replied and asked, what name did he call you? I could hardly say the name again in front of everyone, but after looking at my mother again, I repeated the 'N' word. My mother turned back to the nuns and said, I don't teach my child to hit other students due to name-calling or anything else because these things can be handled differently. I will say that I don't condone, nor should you condone that my child was called the worst name you could ever call another person of color. I believe my daughter reacted out of the magnitude of how this made her feel, along with how our family and ancestors would feel by being called this name. So how would you like to handle this situation? The nuns told my mother they felt I should be suspended for a few days. My heart sank because now I've caused so much trouble for my mother.

My mother, Cynthia Ann Loving, responded to the nuns and said, "Oh no, you will not be suspending my daughter unless you want to be brought up to the board on how you handled this situation." "Do you need me to tell you how damaging the word is?" "Whether my daughter reacted in the wrong manner or not, she will not be suspended. But if you would like to suspend the other child for calling her that name, then I would think that fits the punishment." She went on to add, "Of course you understand that I'm sending my child here to get a great education and the cost of that education shouldn't be for my child to be called Nigger." "This name isn't the same as calling a child something besides their name. This is a name that my family had to hear over and over again as a slave on a daily basis to be degrading to a man or woman of color." "This word alone made them feel less than a human, but nothing more than a slave that couldn't do any better than his master leading him. I would also like to point out this entire school has a total of two black students in attendance. What's going to happen right now is that my child is going back to her classroom to finish her day in school and we will be back at the same time tomorrow." She finished superiorly. The nuns said, "we need to meet with the other parents of the student and get their reaction as well." My mother said in her soft-spoken, yet upper-handed voice, "I completely understand, and if you need me to stay to meet with them and educate them on the meaning of the word, then I will be happy to meet with them as well." "I simply want them to understand; if they have any issues, they can take it up with me. My daughter will not hit anyone ever again unless it's in self-defense. My daughter will not be suspended due to the circumstances." She turned to look at me and said, "Ti'Sha, get your things together and get back to class, so you don't miss any more of your school work today. I love you, and I will see you when you get home today.

I don't know what happened after I left, but when I came home, my mother sat down with me and told me how I handled the situation was wrong, but the other child was wrong for using that hurtful word. My mother told me that she knew that I would never hit anyone just over someone calling me a silly or stupid name, and she felt there had to be more to the story before she arrived to school. Right now, I can't say enough about my mother because she stood up for what she believed but also was able to make me understand things I did wrong. My mother has an easy way to be nice and polite, but to get her point across in every conversation. I will say that I was never in another fight from that point on in my life. I would always think through the situation before reacting and try to discuss the issue with the other person before anything went to the point of any altercation.

She had always given me the ability, to be honest with her about everything in my life. I trusted her completely and never kept things from her, and I know that most kids today wouldn't imagine talking about a lot of things we discussed with our parents. The values and confidence she gave to me are beyond measure. I use all of these tools today to help me in my life. The things she taught me I had to use at an early age because she would soon become ill, and I became her caretaker at an early age. The biggest lesson is for parents to be involved in their kid's daily activities. If the child feels that they can come to talk to you and your reaction will not be one of disappointment or anger, then they might talk to you more often and let you into their world a little more. My mother was always open with her thoughts and never jumped to conclusions before hearing the entire scenario. As a child knowing that you have that comfort of talking with a parent that's open-minded and perhaps will not jump to conclusions, but help you work through the situation is very helpful.

Now, moving forward to the age of 17, I started noticing things that my mother would do that made me wonder, but I would never tell anyone. She was a single mom raising me, and we had other family members, but a lot of the older ones had already passed away when I was in high school. I felt it was really just me and my mother, and we took care of each other. My Grandfather and Grandmother both were diagnosed with mental illnesses, and my mother never wanted to be put in that same category as my grandparents. I understood, and I became the person that she would listen to if she felt something was going wrong in her mind. Sometimes, my mother would ask me if I felt this was something real that had happened, and I would respond, no, mama, that didn't happen. A lot of times, it would help her fight the things in her mind that she was battling on a daily basis. I think the best way to describe a mental illness probably is to watch the movie: 'A Beautiful Mind'; it reminds me of the things my mother went through in her life with one of the most intelligent minds and open hearts that I've ever seen.

At the age of 17, I felt that I needed to get a job in order to help with some of the bills of the house since my mother had retired from teaching and wasn't able to find a steady income after leaving the school. My first job was at Doozer's Burgers and Franks. I was so excited because I thought this would help make a difference with some of our financial problems. Of course, it did help a little, but I wasn't working full-time since I was still in school. In my senior year, things continued to change for my mother, and some days, I couldn't talk her out of things that had entered into her mind. She felt some days that things that had entered into her mind really did happen.

Since this wasn't a daily occurrence or at least I couldn't tell it was a daily occurrence. I would just take the good days with the bad ones. It was almost like my mother was holding on as much as she could in order to see me graduate high school. I believe her mission was to at least see me graduate, and then perhaps she could stop holding back or fighting the crazy enemies that had entered her beautiful mind. As a teenager, I wanted to make sure everything was taken care of for my mother when I graduated high school, but things continued to stay the same. I had been modeling and wanted to continue my big dream of modeling, but with a bigger agency in New York or California. I had a Great Aunt in San Diego and a Great Great Aunt in Los Angeles. They both seemed open to letting us come to California to get a fresh start, and I could focus more on modeling. So, the plan was to pack up and go to California. I felt that we would be able to get back on our feet, and my mother would have more family to help in her situation as well. When we arrived in San Diego, it wasn't quite what we thought, but we were going to make it no matter what happened. After a few months, we still didn't have our own place to live, and my aunt's apartment seemed to be getting smaller and smaller by the minute. I was able to find work as a telemarketer, but it still wasn't enough money to pay a down payment and monthly rent in San Diego. I started to feel like we had made a mistake because I wasn't able to go on any open calls for modeling, and I also needed updated photos to give to agencies. Of course, we didn't give up. My mother was trying to find a job, but between the transportation to and from work and actually finding something seemed to be very difficult. We spoke to my Aunt in Los Angeles, and she wanted us to come to stay with her to see if we would have better luck. My Aunt didn't have any younger kids in the house, and it would probably be easier to find work. We moved to LA, and again, we still had a difficult time finding work. My mother decided that I should stay, and she might have a better time finding work back in Bowling Green. As difficult as it was, she moved back to BG, and I found a job working down the street from my Aunt's house at Del Taco. I loved working at Del Taco, and I think they loved me working there since I was the only person that could speak English. Immediately, I was put on the drive-through orders and taking orders from walk-in customers. I felt like I was starting to find another way that I could actually make this work. I had a full-time position, and when I wasn't working, I was looking up modeling agencies and trying to figure out if I had time to attend any open calls. My first port of call was in LA, and the agents were interested and wanted to see me again with an updated portfolio. I was very excited, and I felt that this was going to work. My concerns for my mother continued to grow because I felt that there wouldn't be anyone to help her through her issues as we would talk through them together.

She ended up moving in with my Grandfather in Bowling Green, which made me feel a little better. As the months passed, I was going back to Bowling Green to be in my best friend's wedding and had planned on returning to LA within a week. Once I came home and attended the wedding, I knew things weren't good between my mother and Grandfather. I felt that someone needed to be there to help. In my mind, I was still thinking that I could accomplish all of these goals, but it's really just me at this point. I told my Aunt in LA that I would be coming back, but it would be later than anticipated. I let my manager at Del Taco know as well what was going on. Things seem to get worse, and none of us seemed to be getting along in the house together. Let me remind you that my Grandfather had been diagnosed with a mental illness a very long time ago, so he was dealing with his issues along with all of us living in the house together. My mother had mental illness but had never been diagnosed, so we were dealing with her issues as well. To say the least, it was a very difficult situation for me to be in at that moment. I remember not telling any of my friends that I never went back to LA. I would try to avoid my friends as much as possible. I wouldn't take their calls, and if I saw one of them from a distance, I would make sure to go in the other direction in hopes that they wouldn't see me. I found a job at a restaurant called 'The China Restaurant' where I started waiting tables. I had no experience except for the fact that I loved Chinese food. I remember thinking about why I had chosen a Chinese Restaurant when I didn't speak Chinese at all? We had two cooks in the kitchen that spoke two different languages, which they couldn't communicate with each other and a manager that could barely speak English. I must say that I learned a lot by working there. It taught me a lot of things about life and different cultures, just as I had also learned working in an all Hispanic Restaurant in Los Angeles. Having limited communication with your manager or the kitchen staff on orders, you learn to communicate in other different ways. I remember learning to speak just enough of their language in order to communicate with them. They taught me a little Chinese and I taught them a little English. My good friend Terry and Leslie were both Asian-Americans, but neither of them spoke any Cantonese. After working at The China Restaurant, I wanted to branch out and try other things. So, I applied for a position at a local and popular Radio Station 93 WKCT. I never thought that I would get the position, but they hired me to run around and take notes and basically be an assistant to all the DJ's. I remember asking questions to my manager, who was the head of the news for the Radio Station, what else I could do to be on the radio? He basically said you need to watch and listen to me when I'm on the air and learn how to take good notes when conducting interviews. One day, he sent me to the courthouse to cover a story about a murder trial. At that time, I had no clue about what I should do to get a sound bite from the attorney. I decided to simply follow the lead of the other reporter and make sure that when she asked questions, my recorder was right next to her. It seemed to work as I got the information I needed for the news story. The next few times, I started to feel confident and was able to start asking questions myself. Within a few months, I was on the radio giving reports with some news spots, obituary, stock market reports. I felt good about this information, and it was giving me the opportunity to do something that I really loved to do. I was working at 93 WKCT Radio Station during the day and then going to The China Restaurant and waiting tables in the evening. My life seemed to be getting back in a direction I wanted it to go. My dreams of modeling still were in my mind, but I felt like I didn't have a lot by being in Bowling Green with limited opportunities for modeling. As I continued to work at the radio station, I ended up meeting a lady by the name of 'Gwen Downs' who was the head of the Human Rights Commission. Gwen seemed to have everything together, and I was impressed with the work she was doing at The Human Rights Commission. After meeting Gwen, she wanted to speak to me about a talk show that aired once a month. The current host was moving out of town and wouldn't be able to continue hosting the show. Gwen asked if I would be interested in taking this position. Honestly, I couldn't believe that I was being asked this question. Of course, I would love to do this for The Human Rights Commission and also be able to have an audience on WBKO13. Again, after accepting the position, I felt overwhelmed. I have a radio position, I was waiting tables at night for The China Restaurant, and now I'm going to be on television? This was such a big step for me, and I wanted to do a good job for the community and not completely fall on my face. My mother was still doing okay with her moments, but she was so proud of the work that I was doing. As I started working and gathering topics and information for the show, I was introduced to Dennis Williams, who was such a wonderful person that also worked for Gwen at The Human Rights Commission. He was always helping me with the topics and making sure my outfit was right on point for the show. One day, Dennis asked me about modeling, and I told him my interest, but just not enough opportunity in Bowling Green. (Let me tell you that God will work things out for you even when you are not expecting anything). Dennis told me that he had a friend who worked as a makeup artist in Louisville at one of the top modeling agencies in Louisville, Ky. I think that I just froze in place in order to remain completely still so I wouldn't pass out on the floor. I really couldn't believe it was happening. All these years, I've looked for an agency, and most of them seemed to be so far away. I'd started to give up on modeling even though it was always in my heart. Dennis said, do you have any headshots I can send to him and see what he thinks? Within a week, I sent him the headshot, and his friend told him that the owner of the agency wanted to meet me. Did a door just open without me knocking? Yes, it did open!

I drove to Louisville to meet the owner, and when I walked in the door, I knew that agency was where I wanted to be. Now, if they would accept me? I walked in the door, and I fell in love. The owner was very upbeat, but I could also tell that she was all about business. Her question to me was if I joined the agency, would I be on time to practice and Go See's like any of the other models that lived in Louisville? She told me that she would expect me to be 30 minutes early to a photoshoot or any Go See, and it didn't matter if I drove two hours to arrive in Louisville along with the time zone change. I agreed I would be early and work late if needed, and I would go to any Go See that she would send me to. For the fashion shows, I told her that I would be at every practice whether I was sick or well because this is something I've always dreamed about doing. Mary J. Kaufman MJK Modeling agency welcomed me into their doors. The team of Jose'ph and Chris Kaufman were amazing! I met so many wonderful people and made lifelong friends and sisters. I will say that to this day; this is the only job that I arrived 30 minutes early each day with a two-hour drive and a time zone change. I was always available for any "Go See", practice show etc... Again, I really needed to be in Louisville, but that wasn't possible at the time. However, when you love something so strongly, it becomes part of who you are and doesn't seem like a job, but it becomes your passion. My message to young people today is never to give up, don't settle! Listen to your heart, and if you stay on the right path, things will come to you. Many lessons I have learned over the years in business, love, family, and friends.

When it comes to love, I was taught never to chase but to stay honest with the person that I am. Love will find me, and I will be able to choose the direction of that love. My husband, Keith Williams, is a Knight in shining honor, and he does everything to make me feel like a woman. I realize that I'm blessed to have a wonderful, caring husband that is truly a blessing to me and our beautiful kids Daymon & Di'Maya. When you are waiting for Mr. Right, I believe that you must figure out a few things first about yourself:

1. You must love yourself
2. Have Self Confidence
3. Understand what you want for your life and for your family

If you are willing to settle for anyone or think that you can change that person, you will be in for a big surprise. If you're not compatible with that person or perhaps you don't have the same vision for your life as your companion does, then you need to stop and evaluate the situation before continuing down that path.

My story of love has been wonderful throughout my life because I learned from each relationship. I can say to this day that I'm friends with my ex-boyfriends. Now don't get me wrong I don't go hanging out with them, but as far as seeing them somewhere and catching up or staying in touch through social media etc. We are still friends, and it's all due to how each relationship ended. Whether it was me or the boyfriend, we would always understand why we needed to go our separate ways and always wished each other the best of luck. Since we couldn't find that compatible partnership with each other, we learned from each other. Everything that you do in one relationship should be a learning experience for the next one. If you go into another relationship without learning from the mistakes of the last one, then you will end up in that same space again. My cousin Dana always asks me if I still have a handbook on relationships since she keeps forgetting to read her handbook. This is a running joke between the two of us because of how hard it is to find a man that you are compatible with, but it's due to the type of signals you send out. The reason I said you need to focus on yourself first is because that's the

key to a great relationship. If you get yourself right, then it will give you more opportunities to attract someone that's more compatible with you.

All of these strong, beautiful, courageous women hopefully through their journey, have touched at least one person that's read this book. During this process of gathering information and asking questions from all of these women, I also was amazed and proud that I was able to put myself in the company of each one. My mother has given me the knowledge and instincts to always make sure I place myself in the midst of people that care and will support me. When I think of my journey, there have been some really great times, and like anyone else, you will always experience challenging times. All of those challenges lead me to Learn, Listen, Lean, Lift, and Love in my Life. Many times, if you do not go through something rough or hard, then you will not learn something that would really make a difference in your life. Experiences in life and learning from them will help you climb to the next level. Listening can be hard without giving your opinion or thinking, "Well, I would've done it like this".

If you can truly listen to the information from another wise person, it will help you improve the steps you take in your journey. I believe that sometimes we dismiss the experiences of our older generation. We must remember our older generation has a wealth of knowledge and experiences that we all can learn from and pass forward to the next generation. Let's start to embrace our older generation on their views and values. You can incorporate some of those core values into your life journey.

Take a minute to uplift someone, you know. This could be done just as easily for a stranger. Giving a compliment and watching someone be uplifted by a small compliment is much more rewarding than not *saying anything at all.*

Be empowered and engaged with LIFE around you. You will miss what's coming your way if you walk with your head looking down. Nothing is going to come your way if you walk with your head looking down. You may be starting from the bottom, but you are climbing your way to the top, so you must always keep your eyes on the prize. Keep your eyes focused on all the things that are up or going up! I promise that it will make a difference in the way you handle daily routines.

Place yourself in the best position to live your best life. In your life, you must understand that all of us were put on this earth for a reason. We are not here because it was an accident. It was meant for you to be here! God makes no mistakes, and once you accept your journey, then you can start writing the path instead of following the path that other people travel. For the longest time, I tried to figure out what I'm supposed to do in life. I would even ask my husband, "What do you think my purpose is in life?" My husband would always say, "you are good at a lot of things, but you are the only one that knows the things that make you happy, which probably includes helping other people while accomplishing your goals."

I feel that accomplishing your goals can be easily attainable with a written plan, a goal-oriented mindset, and working hard toward the goal each and every chance you are able.

I remember when I was growing up, my mother instilled in me at an early age that I could do anything. Of course, every parent feels this way about their child, because you want the best for your child. What you teach your children will help them in their journey. If you tell your child that he or she can do anything, they set their mind to do the impossible. Your children are always watching you. That little human being that you created is looking up to you, watching your every move even when you don't think they are looking. If you have a strong mindset, confidence, and the will to keep trying and never give up, no matter what obstacles may come your way, then they will have that as their example. We should always instill this mindset within our kids. Your child considers you their HERO, and if you are not setting the standard high for yourself, then your child will emulate those standards.

Growing up, I watched my mother, and I wanted to be like her. She was outgoing, intelligent, beautiful, soft-spoken, but strong when speaking her mind. I saw some of the things my mother went through growing up and how she never once gave up on anything. If she liked the dress, but couldn't buy it, then she would look at the dress and write it down on one of her list of goals. While we walked by department stores on our way home, my mother would tell me, "I will be back later to pick up that dress." She would ask me questions like, "where do you want to travel in the United States and outside of the Country?" I would tell her a few states, and then she would say, "When do you want to go?" Sometimes I didn't know what to say, especially with a timeframe, simply because we didn't have any money. To me, these were goals that seem so far away because we didn't have enough money to pay the rent at the time. Little did I know she was preparing me for my journey.

It probably wasn't a month later, and we were able to get back on our feet. My mother went back to the store and bought that dress that had hung in the window for so long. After she bought the dress, she pulled out her piece of paper and marked it off her list. That same year we started traveling with our church group. Within one year, I had been to North Carolina, Mississippi, and Georgia. Basically, what I'm trying to say is that we always need to lead by example with our children.

Those basic mindset rules at age nine continued to stick with me.

That following year I wrote in my diary that I wanted to be able to help my mother, pay for my school, clothes and also buy this beautiful camera that was really out of our budget. Of course, I didn't have a plan, but I knew that I would find a plan to accomplish this goal before the end of the summer. After thinking about it for a few days, I had decided that I would go to the craft store. This store was right around the corner from where my mother worked. My best friend also lived close by, and I went into the craft store and came up with an idea to make cloth macramé owls to hang in the living room. My best friend wasn't really excited, but she agreed to go into business with me. All summer, we made owls, and I sold owls to neighbors, my mother, friends, church groups, or anyone I saw at any time. I made enough money to buy my camera and even had enough to buy some school clothes. The camera became a very important piece in my life. It was the first goal that I met, and I marked it off my list in order to move onto the next goal.

The camera gave me a voice and started to share my journey at age 10. Back 35 years ago, we didn't have social media, but this camera and meeting my goal gave me my voice. It started a path to success and finding my place and purpose in the world a little bit at a time. To this day, I use a camera to share my journey through this book and social media. My last advice and words to you are to:

NEVER GIVE UP.

When others don't think your DREAMS or IDEAS will work, don't let that stop you. Remember, if it was easy, then everyone would be doing the same thing. Don't forget as you continue on your journey to LOVE, LISTEN, LEARN, LIVE, and LAUGH!

SELF CONFIDENCE TIPS

Choose your life partners wisely. Life partners are the people you spend the most time with. Choose your husband, your friends, and your co-workers with this in mind. Surround yourself with positive.

I used to run with doubt. Now she can't keep up with me anymore. God doesn't give us anything we can't handle, and he doesn't expect us to handle it by ourselves. **—Chas Goshorn**

Speaking Life! Let all the words that come from your mouth be positive. **—Shashray McCormack**

Know that you are beautiful no matter what anyone else has to say. KNOW YOU!

Surround yourself with positive people and role models.

Don't dwell on anything you have no control over. Do the best you can and even if the decision you make is a wrong decision. Don't beat yourself up over it. Acknowledge the mistake and move forward. **—Angela Nicole Stevenson**

Create personal affirmations for yourself like, "I love myself unconditionally, and every day in every way I'm getting stronger and stronger." **—Anita Turner**

Take time and look in the mirror don't just pass by. Don't just look at what's on the outside, but take time to examine who you are as a person inside and out. If you don't like what you see, then change it for the better. —**Ti'Sha Loving-Williams**

Don't ever give up or give in. There is a reason you were created, and you can be an inspiration to others. If God brings you to it, He will bring you through it! —**Donna Milton**

I do not know the author of this quote, but it's powerful: Your mind is like your bed you have to make it up everyday and be careful who you let in it! God got it! Unknown —**Selina Gillans**

Viola Davis played an important role in the movie "The Help." She was a Nanny to a lil girl, and each day she would tell her, "You are Good, you are Smart, and you are Important!" Those are words that each one of us should recite to ourselves while looking in a mirror. Believe it, walk in it and live by it. Never allow anyone to make you feel that you are less than! —**Andrea Davis**

Ladies, love yourself and know your worth. Realize that God formed you and knitted you in your mother's womb (Psalms 139:13) and know that you are precious. Take care of yourself, both emotionally and physically. Surround yourself with those who will build you up and not tear you down. Don't give up in hard times. Know that hard times only last for a season and then they will pass and you will be stronger for having endured those hard times. —**Quin Mosley**

Stay positive by thinking everything happens for a reason. Don't be negative toward anything or anyone in life. Make sure you keep positive people in your life. —**Lisa Love Rowe**

Never hold your head down, always look up in the midst of your storm. There's nothing better than being able to see what God has created. It gives you the strength to continue going! Heads Up! —**Ti'Sha Loving-Williams**

The best way to stay positive is to first associate yourself with positive people that will not try to bring you down; they will constantly bring you up. Negative people bring negative energy with them to any place, and to any conversations; misery loves company. They are miserable, and they want you to be miserable like them. When a negative person walks into a room, watch the whole atmosphere just change. If you can avoid it, avoid it at all costs because no one needs it and it's not worth it! You need all the positive people in your life/ lives because they want the very best for you; to succeed in all of your endeavors. I am a very positive person, and I have the best friend you could ever have, and his name is Jesus. I am a strong and steady believer in God, and he is never negative but always positive because his word is true!! —**Chiquita Sparks**

Behind The Mirror

MARRIAGE/DATING TIPS

"You can never truly appreciate love until you've had your heartbroken."

"Don't question yourself. Follow your knee jerk first reaction; it's almost always right" **—Chas Goshorn**

Take care of yourself first. Don't ever depend on any man to take care of or validate you. Have an amazing sense of self and maneuvering through the trials in life will be a little easier. **—Angela Nicole Stevenson**

Marriage must be open and honest communication between two committed individuals. **—Anita Turner**

Marriage is a partnership between two individuals that are compatible with each other and live and believe in the same kind of beliefs. You need to be able to differ, but be on the same page for the bigger picture in life. Talk about what you want for your future with kids, family, religion, and finances while you're dating. If you strongly differ on these four topics, then you might step back and analyze your relationship and make sure it's the right one for you. **—Ti'Sha Loving-Williams**

First of all, I suggest you pray to God, and you should ask God about that particular person. God knows about all of us and whom we are seeking to date. What's meant to be will be and what's not meant to be want be. **—Chiquita Sparks**

Always stay true to yourself and do not allow your need to satisfy others hinder your decisions about YOUR life. The most important thing… WAIT until you are married to have children! That simple. **—Andrea Davis**

The very definition of love is putting the other person's needs before your own. This is EXTREMELY difficult to do, but if both spouses do this, you will have a successful relationship. Make an effort to "stay tuned" to your spouse. After the kids are gone, you don't want to be left with a total stranger. Last, but definitely not least, keep God in your relationship. Look to his word for advice. Corinthians and Ephesians are my "go-to" books for marriage advice and relationship advice in general. I am by no means an expert. I fail every single day. But I'd rather try and fail than fail because I didn't try. **—Quin Mosley**

Keep the word of God in your marriage. Remember to talk and listen to each other. Go to church together and learn about the words of God together. Remain Faithful. Keep it sexy and spicy**! —-Lisa Love Rowe**

My advice to younger women based My on my past experiences; please seek and find and develop a sincere relationship with GOD first, complete High School with a diploma, strive and accomplish as much college education that you can possibly accomplish, marry and plan a family, seek and begin a career of your choice. Lastly, please make sure to take your body into consideration with all check-ups, annuals, and self- mammograms. **—Chiquita Sparks**

PARENTING TIPS

I'm still trying to figure this one out. Children are amazing little gifts that give us a glimpse of what Jesus Christ's heart is like. What I've learned so far is to be consistent. If you say you're going to do something, do it. It's natural for them to want to test your boundaries, but make sure you are clear what will happen if they do and let them know the consequences were their choice. Let them know how loved they are. Tell them that you love them every day and show them. Tell them that God crafted them and that he has a plan for them. Build their confidence at an early age. Teach manners and respect. Saying please, thank you, and saying ma'am and sir will get them farther in life. **—Quin Molsey**

Children need deep roots, and big wings teach them to soar like an eagle! Be the example you want them to see and be! **—Anita Turner**

As we all know, there's no manual that can teach you how to raise your kids, but there's great advice and tips we can all take advice from. Being a parent is the hardest job in the world, but if you understand that the child will not always be a child and that you are the parent to enjoy every step of their development. **—Ti'Sha Loving-Williams**

It's a challenge. Listen to your inner maternal instincts, and don't allow others to tell you how to raise your child. **—Andrea Davis**

Pray for your children, talk to them daily, and Listen to them. **—Karen Stockton**

Stick to your guns. Never make idle threats, say what you mean and not what you say. Give children responsibilities, teach them to be respectful of others and teach them that it is okay to be different. **—Shashray McCormack**

My tip for parenting children is that you're a parent first and then a friend second. Make sure they know the right things. Take them to church. Pray with them. Be the parent you want them to be to their children. **—Lisa Love Rowe**

All I can say, it's trial and error for the simple reason that parenting doesn't come with a book of instructions and neither does children.

You do the best you can with what you have and stay in constant prayer.

Proverbs 22:6, "Train up a child in a way he should go, and when he is old, he will depart from it." Parents love their children all the time, no matter what and how they turn out. **—Chiquita Sparks**

DAILY GOALS

Make sure you set daily goals, no matter how small or how big. Write them down and mark them off as they are accomplished. You will see how wonderful you feel when you mark things off your list of accomplished goals. Your goals can start out as small goals, and then you can increase to the bigger goals later in the process. Each person has a goal and purpose. Start setting them today, no matter how small or how big.

DAILY GOALS - DAY 1

1. _____

2. _____

3. _____

4. _____

5. _____

6. _____

7. _____

8. _____

9. _____

10. _____

Behind The Mirror

DAILY GOALS DAY - 2

1. _____

2. _____

3. _____

4. _____

5. _____

6. _____

7. _____

8. _____

9. _____

10. _____

DAILY GOALS DAY - 3

1. _____

2. _____

3. _____

4. _____

5. _____

6. _____

7. _____

8. _____

9. _____

10. _____

DAILY GOALS DAY - 4

1. _____

2. _____

3. _____

4. _____

5. _____

6. _____

7. _____

8. _____

9. _____

10. _____

DAILY GOALS DAY - 5

1. _____

2. _____

3. _____

4. _____

5. _____

6. _____

7. _____

8. _____

9. _____

10. _____

DAILY GOALS DAY - 6

1. _____

2. _____

3. _____

4. _____

5. _____

6. _____

7. _____

8. _____

9. _____

10. _____

DAILY GOALS DAY 7

1. _____

2. _____

3. _____

4. _____

5. _____

6. _____

7. _____

8. _____

9. _____

10. _____

HEALTH TIPS/EXERCISE TIPS

My healthy tip would be that you can do anything you set out to do in life. During my time of significant weight gain, I was diagnosed with Type 2 diabetes and was ordered to take Glyburide twice a day. I am not one for daily medications, so I began walking every day. Once I felt comfortable enough, I started doing kickboxing, boot camps and weight training. During this time I lost the 49 pounds and have been diabetes-free since the weight loss. **—Angela Nicole Stevenson**

Eat healthy, exercise, drink plenty of water, get sufficient rest and avoid stress as much as possible. **—Andrea Davis**

Remember that a healthy lifestyle consists of eating healthy 80% of the time, and 20% needs to be some form of activity or exercise. If we put items in our bodies that doesn't help our bodies, then no amount of exercise is going to help you lose weight or remain healthy. Drink plenty of water and stick to a workout routine, but make sure you change it up at least every two weeks. Eat healthy foods that consist of fruits and vegetables. Try to lower your carbs as much as you can. Find a healthy lifestyle change that works for you and your daily routine. Stick to the plan because anything you do consistently will add to your good health and years to your life. If you mess up one day and binge on candy don't let that binge take you to a spiral effect. We all have those days. The key is to get back up the next hour and get back focused. Don't wait on starting to be healthy another day. Start that same hour after you messed up. If you continue to procrastinate, then it will continue to happen. If you want to start living healthy, don't wait until Monday to start a healthy routine. Start right at that moment. **—Ti'Sha Loving Williams**

My healthy lifestyle should always have the exercise of some form in a daily routine. I still struggle with my eating habits and also going to the gym on a regular basis. Don't wait on your healthy lifestyle change make the change today. I'm working toward a weight loss goal due to health reasons, but also for my own personal satisfaction. Make the change today before it's necessary due to health reasons. **—Lisa Love Rowe**

DREAMS

Cease the day focus on setting & establishing goals and a life plan for yourself. Don't lose yourself while taking care of others. **—Anita Turner**

Just remember that trouble does not last long. What does not kill you/ break you, only makes you stronger. God gives us trials and tribulations as a test. Keep your eyes on the prize and remember what your goals are. Don't allow anyone or anything to steal your joy. Nobody can change you unless YOU allow them to! **—Andrea Davis**

My advice is to constantly continue to stay positive no matter what. Place all of your trust and confidence in Jesus Christ our Savior because as long as you have him in your life/lives no one or nothing can ever break your confidence or dreams in yourself **—Chiquita Sparks**

You must act now to pursue your dreams. Everything you do on a daily basis must consist of a plan to follow your dreams. If you wait, then you might be too late. **—Ti'Sha Loving Williams**

TELL US YOUR JOURNEY

I would love to hear your journey, and I'm sure several people in the world would love the same. Please submit your journey for a chance to be in the Third Edition of Behind the Mirror Book of Journeys. The submission must be at least a minimum of one page, and the maximum number of pages can be no more than 10 pages. The submission must be based on your journey and also on true events.

Please submit your journey to me through the email below for an opportunity to be in the Third Edition

(behindthemirrorbook@gmail.com)

If we decide to use your journey in our next book, you will be contacted by email. I can't wait to read about your journey and how it can help change someone else's life.

JOURNEYS REVEALED

JOURNEY 1

Cynthia Anne Loving

- Proud Mother to Ti'Sha Loving Williams

- Retired school teacher

- Proud Grandmother to Daymon & Di'Maya

- Graduate of Western Kentucky University

JOURNEY 2

Mary Beth Stevenson Bramer

- An employee of giving back SMILES/Insurance Director

- Wife to Billy Bramer

- Proud mother to Finlee & Step Mother to Gage Bramer

JOURNEY 3

Donna Spillman Milton

- Married to Ricky Milton received a call for a blind date the day of the photoshoot for this book. Married Ricky Milton on May 10, 2015

- Due to reoccurring health issues resigned from Hospice as the Administrative to focus more on health concerns.

- Stepmother to Brooke Bragg, Chris Milton and Step Grandmother to Lanzleee, Ella and Linnox

JOURNEY 4

Chasity Witty Goshorn

- Proud mother to Walker Goshorn & Gunner Goshorn

- Walker is a college student at University of Louisville and Gunner Goshorn student at Greenwood High School

- Happily married for 21 years to Wyatt Goshorn

- Former Event Coordinator for 440 Main Restaurant

- Completed several marathons

- Studied at Western Kentucky University

- Currently working as a Financial Advisor alongside my Father Tony Witty

JOURNEY 5

Angela Nicole Stevenson

- Proud mother to Stephanie Stevenson

- Compliance Specialist Testing for Chase

- Married to Jesus

JOURNEY 6

Shashray McCormack

- Proud wife to Michael Brandon McCormack

- Proud mother of three; Legend, Legacy and Langston

- Teacher for 16 years Bachelors of Science in Health and Human Performance Master's Degree in early childhood education

- Resource Teacher for Jefferson County Public Schools

- Studied at Western Kentucky University

- Studied at University of Louisville

JOURNEY 7

Quintella (Quin) Mosley

- Married to Brian Mosley for 26 years

- Proud mother to 17-year-old Donovan Mosley

- Former Mortgage Loan Officer for 17 years at US Bank

- Currently works for Combined Communications

JOURNEY 8

Kristina Rust

- Married to Chris Rust

- Proud mother to Annabeth Rust

- Graduate from Western Kentucky University

JOURNEY 9

Runnetta Arnold

- Proud mother to Gabrielle Bunton and Josland Arnold.

- Interventional Pain Specialist Receptionist

- "I walk by FAITH not by sight".

JOURNEY 10

Lisa Love Rowe

- Proud mother to Jerrell Michaels Love and Kendra Love

- Former Full-time HOSPICE Aide for Southern Kentucky.

- Former caregiver to my mother Jane Rowe.

- Certified Nursing Assistant

- Board member for a nonprofit that helps youth in the community called Truth in Motion

JOURNEY 11

Chiquita Sparks

- Proud mother to Asa Sparks & Khalin Sparks

- Grandmother to four wonderful kids Jaiden, Za'Mya, Twins Kehlani and Saniyah

- Engaged to be married in 2021

- Bowling Green Human Rights Commission Coordinator

- Administrative Coordinator Fair Housing Outreach Education Coordinator

- Breast Cancer Survivor!

JOURNEY 12

Stevie Dawn Cherry

- Proud wife to Wendell Cherry

- Proud mother to Nathan, Alyssa and Georgia Cherry

- US Bank Business Analyst

JOURNEY 13

Larecia Denning

- Proud mother to Taylor Bell and Braxton Bell

- MBA Western Kentucky University

- Alpha Kappa Alpha Sorority

JOURNEY 14

Selina Gillians

- Proud mother to Deja J. Gillans

- Married to wonderful husband Donovan Gillans

- Bachelor of Arts in Communications

- Masters of Education and Education Specialist Degree in Leadership

- Lead Principal of School Turnaround

JOURNEY 15

Barbara Coleman

- Proud mother of Derrell Coleman and Shadonna Coleman

- Grandmother to six wonderful kids Alyssa Curtis, Talen Lee, Aubrey Malei, Kyrie Young, Jakeyson Young, Tori Jaziel

- Works for General Motors Bowling Green Assembly Plant

JOURNEY 16

Gina Williams

- Proud mother to Christopher Williams

- Owner of Gina's Gorgeous Gems, Creations and Design

- Accounting Specialist Transitioning to become a Lifestyle Trainer and Fitness Coach

- Studied Business Administration at Lindenwood University

JOURNEY 17

Laura Ferguson

- Wife to Robert Ferguson

- Proud mother of two daughters Kaneetha and Monica Step Mother to four Laura, Melissa, Adam and Aaron Ferguson.

- Seven wonderful grandchildren.

- Works at Amerigroup & Travel Consultant at LF Travels

- Owner of 2 Gold Spoons Catering Business

JOURNEY 18

Anita Turner

- Proud mother of three kids Isaiah, Hannah & Hailey Thomas

- Monitor Technician

- BA Psychology from Fisk University

- Presently pursuing RN

JOURNEY 19

Karen Ford Stockton

- Married to wonderful husband Marchel Stockton

- Mother of three Jasmine, Timothy and Faith Stockton

- Grandmother to two wonderful grandchildren Lariea and Nollan Stockton

- Supervisor at a Child Care Facility during the evenings and full-time homemaker during the day

- Lover of GOD all the time

- Firmly believe in acknowledging God in all thine ways, and he shall direct thy path. Proverbs chapter 3 verse 6

JOURNEY 20

Sharon Hayes Blakey

- Married to Barry Blakey

- Proud mother to Vachon Hayes.

- Cake decorator for Country Oven Bakery

- State Street Baptist Church Committees Trustee, Trustee Secretary, Pastor Aide, Pastor Aide Decorator Assistant, Choir Member, Choir Treasurer, Deaconess of the church

- Mime Ministry

- Wedding Planner

JOURNEY 21

Valinda

- Proud mother to Gabrielle and Kyle.

- Senior Management Team at Fruit of the Loom

- Studied at Lincoln U. MO

JOURNEY 22

Anita Michelle Jefferson

- Proud mother to Kamerson and Kendall Ford

- Former Global Support Agent for Fed-Ex

- Associates Degree in Computer Information Systems

- Bachelors in Business and Organizational Management

- Masters in Business Administration

- Due to this journey written almost five years ago, my situation has changed, and my husband joined his heavenly Father in July of 2018.The road has not been easy, and I deal with daily struggles of grief, but I understand that God has a reason for everything, and this is another chapter in my journey. God allowed us to find each other and love each other in a short period of time. We grew together and learned from one another. My husband, William Patton is now an angel watching over me.

Cecilia Loving Cromwell

- Married to Marlon Cromwell

- Spiritual Leader at God is a Brown Girl Too

- Deputy Commissioner at NYC Fire Department

- Author of the following books, God's A Brown Girl Too, Prayers for those standing on the edge of greatness, Seeing myself as God sees me, God is a Lawyer Too

JOURNEY 24

Andrea Patton Brantley

- Proud wife to Robert Brantley for 24 years

- Proud mother to my sons Trace, Ty & Tucker

- Licensed Funeral Director and Manager of family owned business Patton Funeral Home

- Graduate of Western Kentucky University

- Bachelor of Arts Degree in Public Relations and Marketing

JOURNEY 25

Andrea Davis

- Proud Mother of Ayden

- Owner of Klassy Tee

- Graduate of Western Kentucky University

JOURNEY 26

Ti'Sha Loving Williams

- Author of Behind the Mirror

- Proud daughter of Cynthia Anne Loving

- Proud Mother to Daymon & Di'Maya Williams

- Married to my best friend Keith Williams for 19 years

- Proud member of Next Level Church Bowling Green Kentucky

- US Bank Sales Manager for 25 years

- Proud friend to all of these wonderful women in my life

Behind The Mirror

204   Behind The Mirror

Behind The Mirror

I AM FEARLESS

I AM POWERFUL

I AM BEAUTY

I AM HAPPINESS

I AM INTELLIGENT

I AM STRONG

I AM LISTENING

I AM LOVE

I AM LOVING

I AM TRUTH

I AM FLAWLESS

I AM SIMPLE

I AM HONESTY

I AM BOLD

I AM CONFIDENT

I AM LIMITLESS

I AM EMPOWERING

I AM EMPATHETIC

I AM PRETTY

I AM HUMANKIND

I AM MY SISTERS KEEPER

I AM A WOMAN

I AM REASONABLE

I AM PRICELESS

I AM COURAGEOUS

I AM SMART

I AM MAGNIFICENT

I AM BLESSED

I AM A MOTHER

I AM YOUR SISTER

I AM FRIENDLY

I AM VALUABLE

I AM BRAVE

I AM A LEADER

I AM HEALTHY

I AM A QUEEN

I AM BODY IMAGE

I AM HEALTHY

I AM RICH

I AM KINDNESS

I AM LOVEABLE

I AM MAJESTIC

I AM OPEN MINDED

I AM UNIQUE

I AM TEACHABLE

I AM ALIVE

I AM A SURVIVOR

I AM A FIGHTER

I AM TIMELESS

I AM HERE FOR A REASON

I AM TRUTH

I AM RELIABLE

I AM UNDERSTANDING

I AM LOYAL

I AM TREMENDOUS

I AM UNBREAKABLE

I AM AMAZING

I AM GRATEFUL

I AM POSSIBLE

I AM WOKE

I AM WISE

I AM UNTOUCHABLE

I AM RESPONSIBLE

I AM DEDICATED

I AM CREATIVE

I AM ENOUGH!

*I'm dedicating this book in the honor of
my Grandmother Geneva Hitchens Loving,
my Mother Cynthia Loving and
my Mother In Law Bertie Williams*